Trevor Senior

Exam Practice Workbook

AQA
GCSE Maths
Foundation Tier

Contents

Contents

STATISTICS & PROBABILITY

N.B. Questions indicated with an asterisk (*) are ones where the quality of your written communication (QWC) will be assessed.

Where any questions are labelled with the symbol 🖩, attempt all parts of the question without a calculator.

NUMBER & ALGEBRA

Basic Number Work

1. (a) Write the number 3025 in words.

Answer: _____ *(1 mark)*

(b) Write the number two thousand and nine in digits.

Answer: _____ *(1 mark)*

2. Fifty-five people go out for a meal at a restaurant. Each table seats four people.

How many tables are needed?

_____

Answer: _____ *(3 marks)*

3. (a) What is the value of the digit 6 in the number 4601?

Answer: _____ *(1 mark)*

(b) Work out 187×32

_____

_____

Answer: _____ *(3 marks)*

4. Work out:

(a) $257 + 196$

_____

Answer: _____ *(1 mark)*

(b) $491 - 129$

_____

Answer: _____ *(1 mark)*

(c) 15×63

_____

Answer: _____ *(1 mark)*

(d) $875 \div 5$

_____

Answer: _____ *(1 mark)*

5. Here are six numbers:

25   43   48   57   63   71

(a) Which two numbers add up to 120?

Answer: .... *(1 mark)*

(b) Which two numbers have a difference of 38?

Answer: .... *(1 mark)*

(c) What is the biggest answer possible when two of the numbers are multiplied together?

Answer: .... *(1 mark)*

6. Here are six numbers:

5   11   29   41   52   60

(a) Which two numbers add up to 70?

Answer: .... *(1 mark)*

(b) Which two numbers when multiplied together give an answer of 319?

Answer: .... *(1 mark)*

(c) What is the smallest answer possible when two of the numbers are multiplied together?

Answer: .... *(1 mark)*

7. Mr Jones uses 1328 units of gas. Each unit costs 15.5p. Work out the total cost of the units of gas used.

Answer: £ .... *(3 marks)*

(Total: .... / 22 marks)

Positive and Negative Numbers

1. The temperature at midnight was −3°C. By 6am the temperature had fallen by 4°C.

What is the temperature at 6am?

_____

Answer: _____ °C   *(1 mark)*

2. ***(a)** Here is a bank statement. Complete the balance column.

Date	Description	Credits	Debits	Balance
08/07/12				£530.20
09/07/12	Gas bill		£102.15	
10/07/12	Supermarket		£60.80	
12/07/12	Wage	£420.65		

(3 marks)

(b) What would a negative number in the balance column mean?

_____
(1 mark)

3. Work out:

(a) −3 − (−2)

_____

Answer: _____   *(1 mark)*

(b) 8 × −6

_____

Answer: _____   *(1 mark)*

(c) −84 ÷ −7

_____

Answer: _____   *(1 mark)*

4. In this magic square every row, column and diagonal adds up to 0.

Fill in the missing numbers.

3	−4	
	0	

(2 marks)

5. The temperature on Venus is 480°C.

The temperature on Jupiter is −150°C.

(a) Work out the difference in temperature between Venus and Jupiter.

Answer: ....°C   *(1 mark)*

(b) The temperature on Saturn is 30°C lower than on Jupiter.

Work out the temperature on Saturn.

Answer: ....°C   *(1 mark)*

6. Here are six numbers:

5   −5   3   −3   2   −2

(a) Which two numbers when added together give the lowest answer?

Answer: ....   *(1 mark)*

(b) Which two numbers when multiplied together give the lowest answer?

Answer: ....   *(1 mark)*

(c) What is the difference between the lowest and highest of these numbers?

Answer: ....   *(2 marks)*

(Total: .... / 16 marks)

Rounding

1. Use approximations to estimate the value of 39×302

Answer: _____ *(2 marks)*

2. Estimate the value of 98×5.1

Answer: _____ *(2 marks)*

3. Boxes of chocolate cost £2.49 each. Estimate the number of boxes I can buy for £20.

Answer: _____ *(2 marks)*

4. Work out 18.4×7.3

(a) Write down all the figures on your calculator display.

Answer: _____ *(1 mark)*

(b) Give your answer to 1 decimal place.

Answer: _____ *(1 mark)*

5. Work out $\dfrac{8.34 + 7.12}{3.5 \times 1.2}$

(a) Write down all the figures on your calculator display.

Answer: _____ *(1 mark)*

(b) Give your answer to 1 decimal place.

Answer: _____ *(1 mark)*

6. Use your calculator to work out the value of $\sqrt{29.71 - 5.2^2}$

(a) Give your answer as a decimal. Write down all the figures on your calculator display.

Answer: _____ *(1 mark)*

(b) Give your answer to 1 significant figure.

Answer: _____ *(1 mark)*

7. Use your calculator to work out $32^2 + \sqrt{4500}$

(a) Give your answer as a decimal. Write down all the figures on your calculator display.

Answer: _____ *(1 mark)*

(b) Give your answer to 1 significant figure.

Answer: _____ *(1 mark)*

8. A lorry load of recycled waste weighs 19.7 tonnes. It is worth £30.50 per tonne.

Approximately how much is it worth?

Answer: £ _____ *(2 marks)*

9. A car travels at 68 miles per hour for 1 hour 55 minutes.

Approximately how far does it travel?

Answer: _____ miles *(2 marks)*

10. Use approximations to estimate the value of $\dfrac{198 \times 51}{39}$

Answer: _____ *(2 marks)*

*11. Alf and Bob used calculators to work out $\dfrac{36.41}{10.3 \times 0.21}$ to 1 decimal place.

Alf's answer was 16.8

Bob's answer was 0.74

Use approximations to find out who was correct.

Answer: _____ *(3 marks)*

(Total: _____ / 23 marks)

Multiples and Factors

1. Here is a list of numbers:

   6   8   10   12   15   17   32

   From the list, write down:

   (a) an odd number.

   Answer: _____   *(1 mark)*

   (b) a multiple of 5.

   Answer: _____   *(1 mark)*

   (c) a factor of 16.

   Answer: _____   *(1 mark)*

   (d) a prime number.

   Answer: _____   *(1 mark)*

2. **(a)** Work out the value of $2 + 4 \times 3$

   _____

   Answer: _____   *(2 marks)*

   (b) Work out the value of $5^2 - 3^2$

   _____

   Answer: _____   *(2 marks)*

*3. Bread rolls are sold in packs of 12. Burgers are sold in packs of 10.

   How many packs of each are needed to have the same number of bread rolls and burgers?

   _____

   _____

   Answer: _____   *(3 marks)*

4. Emily writes down all the multiples of 6 that are less than 50.

   Starla writes down all the multiples of 8 that are less than 50.

   Which numbers are in both lists?

   _____

   _____

   Answer: _____   *(3 marks)*

5. I have two alarms that both go off at 7am. The first alarm repeats every 30 seconds. The second alarm repeats every 40 seconds.

How long is it before they both go off together again?

Answer: .... *(3 marks)*

6. I am thinking of a number between 20 and 40. It is a multiple of 9. It is a factor of 72.

What number am I thinking of?

Answer: .... *(3 marks)*

7. As a product of its prime factors $36 = 2^2 \times 3^2$

(a) Work out the least common multiple (LCM) of 36 and 24.

Answer: .... *(2 marks)*

(b) Work out the highest common factor (HCF) of 36 and 60.

Answer: .... *(2 marks)*

8. Express 96 as a product of prime factors. Give your answer in index form.

Answer: .... *(3 marks)*

(Total: .... / 27 marks)

Fractions

 1. **(a)** Shade $\frac{3}{4}$ of this shape.

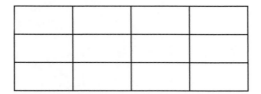

(1 mark)

(b) Write down the fraction of this shape that is shaded. Write your fraction in its simplest form.

Answer: .... *(2 marks)*

 2. Work out $\frac{1}{2} - \frac{1}{5}$

Answer: .... *(2 marks)*

 3. Put these fractions in order, starting with the smallest.

$$\frac{3}{4} \qquad \frac{2}{3} \qquad \frac{5}{6}$$

Answer: .... *(2 marks)*

4. 360 people attend a concert. $\frac{1}{3}$ of these people are men. $\frac{3}{10}$ of these people are women.

Work out the number of children at the concert.

Answer: .... *(3 marks)*

 5. A shirt is normally priced at £28. In a sale it has $\frac{1}{4}$ off the normal price.

Work out the cost of the shirt in the sale.

Answer: £ .... *(2 marks)*

6. Work out $\frac{2}{5} \times 4$. Give your answer as a mixed number.

Answer: .... *(2 marks)*

7. In a class of 30 students, 12 are girls. One-third of the boys study history.

What fraction of the class are boys who study history? Give your answer as a fraction in its simplest form.

Answer: .... *(3 marks)*

*8. Which is bigger, $\frac{2}{3}$ of 45 or $\frac{3}{4}$ of 44?

Answer: .... *(3 marks)*

*9. Which is the better score, 18 out of 30 or 13 out of 20?

Answer: .... *(3 marks)*

*10. Matt buys two bags of potatoes. One bag weighs $2\frac{1}{4}$ kilograms. The other bag weighs $3\frac{2}{3}$ kilograms.

Matt says he has over 6 kilograms of potatoes.

Is he correct? Show clearly how you work out your answer.

.... *(4 marks)*

(Total: .... / 27 marks)

Decimals

1. Write these decimals in order, starting with the smallest.

81.7   80.9   89.0   87.1   81.07

Answer: _____ *(2 marks)*

2. **(a)** Work out 5.3 + 2.8

Answer: _____ *(1 mark)*

(b) Work out 7.1 − 3.5

Answer: _____ *(1 mark)*

3. Natasha buys a chocolate cake for £2.49. She now has £8.60 left in her purse.

(a) How much did Natasha have before she bought the cake?

_____

Answer: £ _____ *(1 mark)*

(b) She then buys a loaf for £1.15. How much has she now?

_____

Answer: £ _____ *(1 mark)*

4. **(a)** Complete Mandy's shopping bill.

3 apples at 45p each	_____
1 pack of sausages	£1.50
2 loaves at £1.15 each	_____
Total	_____

(3 marks)

(b) How much change should Mandy get from a £10 note?

_____

Answer: £ _____ *(1 mark)*

5. Fill in the missing values.

(a) 3.4 + _____ = 5.9 *(1 mark)*

(b) 8.2 − _____ = 4.7 *(1 mark)*

(c) 0.2 × _____ = 0.06 *(1 mark)*

6. What number is halfway between 3.6 and 4.9?

Answer: .... *(2 marks)*

*7. Belinda went shopping. She saw these items that she wanted to buy:

CD   Book   Blouse   Gift Set

£5.95   £9.45   £19.50   £14.75
             True
             Stories

She only bought two of the items. She spent £24.20. Which two items did she buy?

You **must** show how you worked out your answer.

(3 marks)

8. Change $\frac{5}{8}$ to a decimal.

Answer: .... *(2 marks)*

9. Work out $8.4 - 2 \times 1.5$

Answer: .... *(2 marks)*

10. The ticket prices for a cinema are shown.

Adult	£8.70
Child	£5.40
Family ticket (2 adults and 2 children)	£22.50

How much would a family of two adults and two children save by buying a family ticket?

Answer: £ .... *(3 marks)*

(Total: .... / 25 marks)

Percentages

1. Complete the table.

Percentage	Fraction	Decimal
25%		
	$\frac{3}{10}$	
		0.75

(3 marks)

2. Convert 32% to a fraction in its simplest form.

Answer: _____ (2 marks)

3. Jack scored 35 out of 60 in a test. Convert this score to a percentage.

Answer: _____ % (2 marks)

4. David's pay is £15 000 per year. He saves 8% of his pay each month.

How much does he save each month?

Answer: £ _____ (3 marks)

*5. These two adverts are for the same TV. Which company is cheaper?

TV Retail
£350 plus
VAT at 20%

My TV
Normal price:
£560 including VAT
Special offer:
30% off

Answer: _____ (4 marks)

6. A dress is reduced from £60 to £35 in a sale. Work out the percentage reduction.

Answer: .... %　　　　　　　　　　　　　　*(3 marks)*

7. How many grams of cereal are in the box?

Normally 500 grams, 20% extra

Wheatyflakes

Answer: .... grams　　　　　　　　　　*(3 marks)*

*8. Mr Bull bought some shares for £5000. The value of the shares increased by 15%. He then sold some of his shares for £2000. The value of his remaining shares then decreased by 18%.

Overall, has he made a profit or a loss? Show clearly how you obtain your answer.

Answer: ....　　　　　　　　　　　　　*(5 marks)*

*9. Rosie and Jason both took two tests. Both tests are out of the same mark.

	Test 1	Test 2
Rosie	16	19
Jason	14	18

Whose result had the greater percentage increase? You **must** show your working.

Answer: ....　　　　　　　　　　　　　*(3 marks)*

(Total: .... / 28 marks)

Powers and Roots

1. **(a)** Write down the value of 13^2.

Answer: _____ *(1 mark)*

(b) Write down the value of 5^3.

Answer: _____ *(1 mark)*

2. Use your calculator to work out:

(a) 23^2

Answer: _____ *(1 mark)*

(b) 8.9^3

Answer: _____ *(1 mark)*

3. I am thinking of a square number. It is between 80 and 90.

What number am I thinking of?

Answer: _____ *(1 mark)*

4. **(a)** Write down the value of $\sqrt{121}$

Answer: _____ *(1 mark)*

(b) Write down the value of $\sqrt[3]{27}$

Answer: _____ *(1 mark)*

*5. Which is bigger, 4^2 or 2^3? Show clearly how you decide.

_____

_____

Answer: _____ *(3 marks)*

6. **(a)** Write $2^4 \times 2^5$ as a single power of 2.

Answer: _____ *(1 mark)*

(b) Write $3^8 \div 3^4$ as a single power of 3.

Answer: _____ *(1 mark)*

(c) Work out the value of $\dfrac{5^4 \times 5^2}{5^3}$

_____

_____

Answer: _____ *(2 marks)*

7. **(a)** Write $6^2 \times 6^4$ as a single power of 6.

Answer: _____ *(1 mark)*

(b) Write $5^8 \div 5^2$ as a single power of 5.

Answer: _____ *(1 mark)*

(c) Write down the value of 7^1.

Answer: _____ *(1 mark)*

8. **(a)** Write down the value of 14^2.

Answer: _____ *(1 mark)*

(b) Use your answer to part **(a)** to write down the value of 1.4^2

Answer: _____ *(1 mark)*

9. **(a)** Write 16 as a power of 2.

Answer: _____ *(1 mark)*

(b) Write 16×2^3 as a power of 2.

Answer: _____ *(1 mark)*

*10. Which of these is the odd one out?

$$64^1 \qquad 8^2 \qquad 4^3 \qquad 2^4$$

Show clearly how you got your answer.

Answer: _____ *(3 marks)*

(Total: _____ / 24 marks)

Ratio

1.   **(a)** Write the ratio 32 : 8 in its simplest form.

Answer: _____ : _____   *(1 mark)*

(b) Write the ratio 1.25 kg : 250 g in its simplest form.

_____

Answer: _____ : _____   *(2 marks)*

2.   A map has a scale of 1 cm : 4 km. Write this scale as a ratio in its simplest form.

_____

_____

Answer: _____ : _____   *(3 marks)*

3.   Divide £60 in the ratio 2 : 1

_____

Answer: _____ : _____   *(2 marks)*

4.   Divide £85 in the ratio 3 : 2

_____

_____

Answer: _____ : _____   *(3 marks)*

5.   Divide 140 grams in the ratio 2 : 5

_____

_____

Answer: _____ : _____   *(3 marks)*

6.   Divide 63 grams in the ratio 2 : 3 : 4

_____

_____

Answer: _____ : _____ : _____   *(3 marks)*

7. £35 is shared between Ann and Ben in the ratio 2 : 5

How much more does Ben get than Ann?

Answer: £ .... (3 marks)

8. A shop mixes pink paint using red paint and white paint in the ratio 1 : 5

How much white paint is needed to mix a 750 ml tin of pink paint?

Answer: .... ml (3 marks)

9. Andy makes mortar to build a wall. He mixes sand and cement in the ratio 4 : 1

What percentage of the mortar is sand?

Answer: .... % (2 marks)

10. John had £120. He gave $\frac{2}{3}$ of the £120 to his sister. His sister shared this money between her two children in the ratio 3 : 5. How much was the larger share?

Answer: £ .... (3 marks)

11. There are 180 passengers on a train. Standard-class passengers : First-class passengers = 7 : 2

The average cost of a standard-fare ticket is £38. The average cost of a first-class ticket is £54.

Work out the amount of money taken in ticket sales.

Answer: £ .... (5 marks)

(Total: .... / 33 marks)

Proportion

1. Here is a recipe for a sponge cake for six people:

180 grams butter	120 grams jam
180 grams flour	90 ml cream
180 grams caster sugar	3 eggs

How much of each ingredient will be needed to make a cake for four people?

Complete the table.

_____	grams butter	_____	grams jam
_____	grams flour	_____	ml cream
_____	grams caster sugar	_____	eggs

(4 marks)

*2. A recipe for 20 biscuits uses 100 grams of butter and 250 grams of flour. Jean only has 75 grams of butter and 150 grams of flour. What is the maximum number of biscuits she could make?

....

....

Answer: .... *(3 marks)*

3. A car travels 120 miles in 2.5 hours. Work out the average speed in miles per hour.

....

....

Answer: .... mph *(2 marks)*

4. £1 = $1.55

(a) Convert £500 to dollars ($).

....

....

Answer: $ .... *(2 marks)*

(b) Convert $900 to pounds (£).

....

....

Answer: £ .... *(2 marks)*

*5. Which is the best buy? You **must** show all your working.

Answer: .... *(3 marks)*

*6. Which box of eggs is the better value? You **must** show all your working.

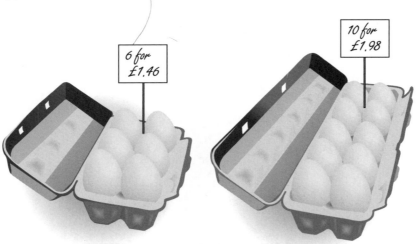

Answer: .... *(3 marks)*

(Total: .... / 19 marks)

Basic Algebra

1. **(a)** Write down an expression that is 5 more than x.

    Answer: _____   *(1 mark)*

    (b) Write down an expression that is one-third of y.

    Answer: _____   *(1 mark)*

2. The rule to convert miles to kilometres is: *Divide by 5 and then multiply by 8*

    (a) Convert 15 miles to kilometres.

    _____

    Answer: _____ km   *(2 marks)*

    (b) Convert 60 kilometres to miles.

    _____

    Answer: _____ miles   *(2 marks)*

3. You are given that: *Time in New York = Time in London – 5 hours*

    (a) What time is it in New York when it is 2pm in London?

    Answer: _____   *(1 mark)*

    (b) What time is it in London when it is 11.45pm in New York?

    Answer: _____   *(1 mark)*

4. **(a)** Simplify $5x - 4x + 6x$

    Answer: _____   *(1 mark)*

    (b) Simplify $11x + 23y - 18x - 14y$

    _____

    Answer: _____   *(2 marks)*

5. Decide if each of the following is an **expression**, **equation** or **formula**.

    (a) $5x - 4 = 11$

    Answer: _____   *(1 mark)*

    (b) $A = l \times w$

    Answer: _____   *(1 mark)*

    (c) $3x + 1$

    Answer: _____   *(1 mark)*

6. $x = 5$ and $y = -2$

(a) Work out the value of $2x - 3y$

Answer: _____ *(2 marks)*

(b) Work out the value of $x^2 - y^2$

Answer: _____ *(3 marks)*

7. Work out values for a and b so that $3x + 4y - 5x + 8y = ax + by$

Answer: $a =$ _____ $b =$ _____ *(2 marks)*

8. n is a positive integer. Decide whether $5n + 3$ is always even, always odd or could be either odd or even.

Answer: _____ *(2 marks)*

9. p is an odd number and q is an even number. Decide whether each of the following is **odd** or **even**.

(a) $p + q$

Answer: _____ *(1 mark)*

(b) pq

Answer: _____ *(1 mark)*

(c) $2p + q$

Answer: _____ *(1 mark)*

10. Make x the subject of $y = 5x - 6$

Answer: _____ *(2 marks)*

(Total: _____ / 28 marks)

NUMBER & ALGEBRA

1. Multiply out $3(x - 6)$

Answer: _____ (1 mark)

2. Multiply out $x(x + 4)$

Answer: _____ (1 mark)

3. Expand and simplify $2(x - 1) + 3(x + 3)$

Answer: _____ (2 marks)

4. Expand and simplify $7(2x + 3) - 2(2x - 3)$

Answer: _____ (2 marks)

5. Factorise $5x - 10$

Answer: _____ (1 mark)

6. Factorise fully $3x^2 + 6x$

Answer: _____ (2 marks)

7. Factorise $8x + 10$

Answer: _____ (1 mark)

8. Factorise fully $5xy - 20y^2$

Answer: _____ (2 marks)

9. John is asked to factorise fully $4x^2 + 8xy$

He writes $2x(2x + 4y)$

Explain the mistake that he has made, showing clearly the correct answer.

Answer: .... *(1 mark)*

10. The equation $x^3 + x = 20$ has a solution between 2 and 3.

Find this solution and give your answer to 1 decimal place.

You **must** show all your working.

Answer: .... *(4 marks)*

11. Use trial and improvement to find an approximate solution to $x^3 - 3x = 30$

Give your answer to 1 decimal place. You **must** show all your working.

Answer: .... *(4 marks)*

(Total: .... / 21 marks)

Linear Equations

1. **(a)** Solve $x - 8 = 14$

   $x =$ _____ *(1 mark)*

   (b) Solve $9x = 27$

   $x =$ _____ *(1 mark)*

2. **(a)** Solve $7x - 5 = 23$

   $x =$ _____ *(2 marks)*

   (b) Solve $3x + 4 = x + 5$

   $x =$ _____ *(2 marks)*

3. **(a)** Solve $5x + 6 = 2x - 15$

   $x =$ _____ *(2 marks)*

   (b) Solve $4(2x - 1) = 28$

   $x =$ _____ *(3 marks)*

4. Solve $\dfrac{x}{2} + 5 = 9$

   $x =$ _____ *(2 marks)*

5. Bob is thinking of a number. He multiplies it by 4 and then subtracts 7. Vic is thinking of the same number. He multiplies it by 3 and then adds 5. They both get the same answer.

What number did they think of?

Answer: .... *(3 marks)*

6. I am x years old. I am 28 years older than my son. In five years' time I will be twice as old as my son.

How old am I now?

Answer: .... *(5 marks)*

*7. Here is a triangle:

Not drawn accurately

$x + 60°$

$3x$

$2x$

Work out the size of the largest angle.

Answer: .... degrees *(4 marks)*

(Total: .... / 25 marks)

Patterns and Sequences

1. Here is a pattern made from sticks:

(a) Draw the next pattern on a separate piece of paper. *(1 mark)*

(b) How many sticks are in the sixth pattern?

_____

Answer: _____ *(1 mark)*

(c) I have 50 sticks. How many sticks will I have left over if I make the biggest possible pattern?

_____

Answer: _____ *(2 marks)*

2. Here is a sequence: 13   17   21   25   29

(a) Write down the next two numbers in the sequence.

_____

Answer: _____ *(2 marks)*

(b) Write down the rule for continuing the sequence.

Answer: _____ *(1 mark)*

3. Here are the first five terms of a sequence: 22   18   14   10   6

(a) Write down the next two numbers in the sequence.

_____

Answer: _____ *(2 marks)*

(b) Write down the rule for continuing the sequence.

Answer: _____ *(1 mark)*

4. Here are the first five terms of a sequence: 7   10   13   16   19

(a) Find, in terms of n, an expression for the nth term of the sequence.

_____

Answer: _____ *(2 marks)*

(b) Michelle says that 152 is a term in this sequence. Explain why she is wrong.

_____ *(1 mark)*

5. The nth term of a sequence is $5n - 3$.

(a) Find the sixth term of the sequence.

Answer: ....

(2 marks)

(b) Is the number 85 a term of the sequence? Give a reason for your answer.

(1 mark)

6. A shopkeeper starts building a display as shown.
He will use 28 tins altogether.

How many tins are in the bottom layer when all 28 tins are used? You **must** show your working.

Answer: ....

(2 marks)

7. Here is a sequence of patterns made from white and shaded circles:

Pattern 1   Pattern 2   Pattern 3

(a) How many white circles are in the nth pattern?

Answer: ....

(2 marks)

(b) How many circles altogether are in the nth pattern?

Answer: ....

(2 marks)

(Total: .... / 22 marks)

Straight Line Graphs

1. **(a)** Complete the table of values for $y = 3x - 4$

x	−2	−1	0	1	2
y	−10		−4	−1	

(1 mark)

(b) Draw the graph of $y = 3x - 4$ for values of x from −2 to 2.

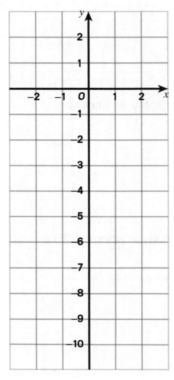

(2 marks)

2. Draw the graph of $y = 2x + 1$ for values of x from −2 to 2.

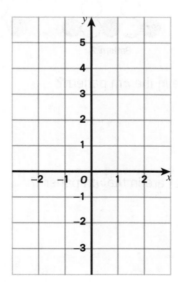

(3 marks)

3. Draw the graph of $x + y = 4$ for values of x from 0 to 4.

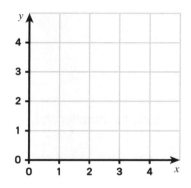

(3 marks)

4. **(a)** Plot the points A (0, 2) and B (4, 10) on the grid.

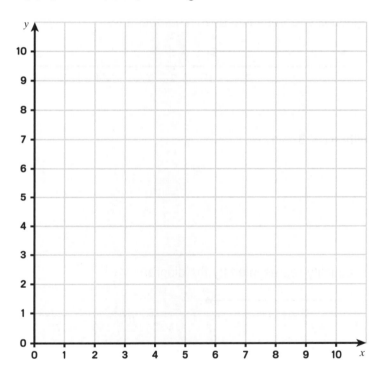

(2 marks)

(b) Join the points A and B. *(1 mark)*

(c) Work out the gradient of the line that passes through A and B.

Answer: .... *(2 marks)*

(Total: .... **/ 14 marks)**

Linear Inequalities and Quadratic Graphs

1. **(a)** Solve $2x + 1 < 7$

Answer: _____ (2 marks)

(b) Represent the inequality $2 \leqslant x < 5$ on the number line.

(2 marks)

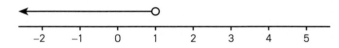

2. **(a)** Write down the inequality represented by this number line.

Answer: _____ (1 mark)

(b) Solve the inequality $4x - 3 \leqslant 17$

Answer: _____ (2 marks)

3. **(a)** Write down the inequality represented by the diagram.

Answer: _____ (1 mark)

(b) Write down the integer values satisfied by the inequality $-1 < x \leqslant 2$

Answer: _____ (2 marks)

4. I have £3.50 to spend on new light bulbs costing £x each. I can afford to buy three bulbs. I cannot afford to buy four bulbs.

(a) Explain why $3x \leqslant 3.50$

_____ (1 mark)

(b) Explain why $4x > 3.50$

_____ (1 mark)

(c) Work out the maximum possible price of one bulb.

Answer: £ .... *(2 marks)*

5. **(a)** Complete the table of values for $y = x^2 + 2$

x	−2	−1	0	1	2
y	6			3	

(2 marks)

(b) On the grid draw the graph of $y = x^2 + 2$

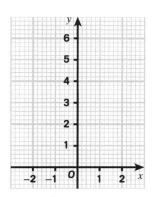

(2 marks)

6. **(a)** Complete the table of values for $y = x^2 - 2x$

x	−1	0	1	2	3	4
y			−1		3	8

(2 marks)

(b) On the grid draw the graph of $y = x^2 - 2x$ for values of x from −1 to 4.

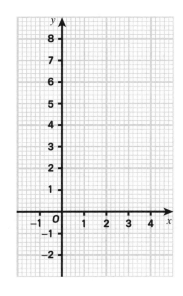

(2 marks)

(Total: ..../ **22 marks)**

Real-life Graphs

1. You are given that 10 kilograms = 22 pounds

(a) Complete this table.

Kilograms	0	10	20
Pounds	0		

(1 mark)

(b) On the grid draw a graph to convert kilograms to pounds.

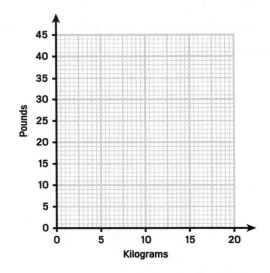

(2 marks)

(c) Use the graph to convert 14 kilograms to pounds.

Answer: _____ pounds

(1 mark)

*(d) Which is greater, 18 kilograms or 37 pounds? You **must** show your working.

_____

Answer: _____

(3 marks)

2. The following graph can be used to convert between centimetres and inches.

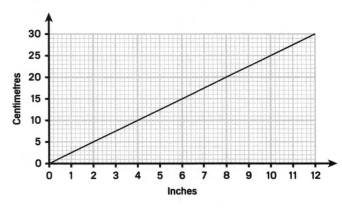

(a) Convert 10 inches to centimetres.

Answer: _____ cm

(1 mark)

(b) There are 12 inches in 1 foot. Use your answer to part **(a)** to convert 5 feet into centimetres.

Answer: _____ cm   *(3 marks)*

3. The distance–time graph shows Tom's journey from home to a relative's flat and back home.

(a) How far does the relative live from Tom's home?

Answer: _____ miles

(1 mark)

(b) How long does Tom spend at the relative's flat?

Answer: _____ hours

(1 mark)

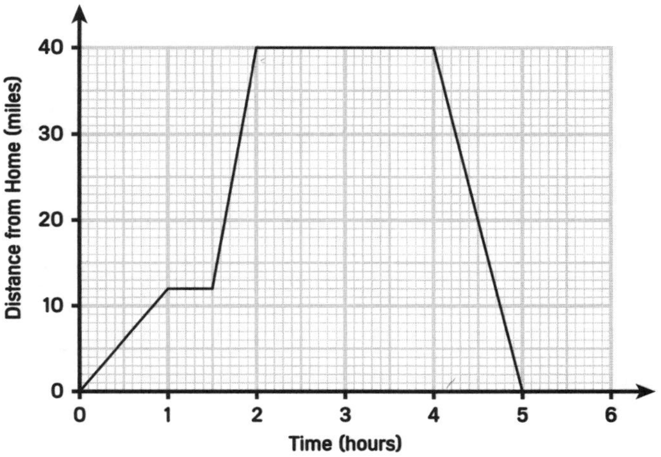

4. The graph shows a 400-metre race between Usain, Ben and Carl.

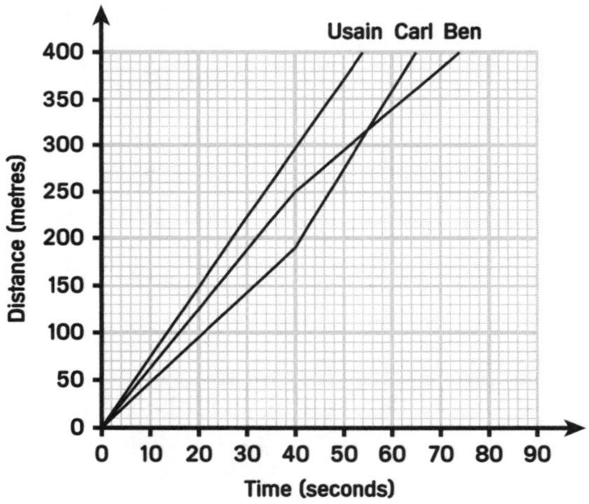

(a) In what order do they finish the race?

Answer: _____   *(1 mark)*

(b) Describe what happened during the race.

(3 marks)

(Total: _____ / 17 marks)

Symmetry and Shapes

1. **(a)** Complete the shape so that it has line symmetry about the mirror line.

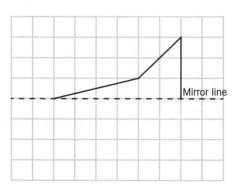

(1 mark)

(b) Complete the shape so that it has line symmetry about both mirror lines.

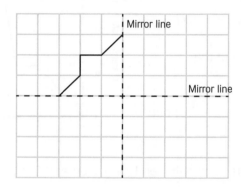

(2 marks)

2. State the order of rotational symmetry of each of these shapes.

Shape A	Shape B	Shape C

Answer: _____   _____   _____   (3 marks)

3. **(a)** Shade **two** more squares so that the grid has one line of symmetry.

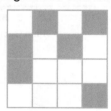

(2 marks)

(b) Shade **two** more squares so that this grid has rotational symmetry of order 2.

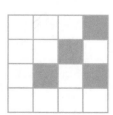

(2 marks)

4. **(a)** What is the name of this type of triangle?

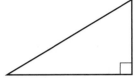

Answer: _____ *(1 mark)*

(b) What is the name of this type of quadrilateral?

Answer: _____ *(1 mark)*

 5. On the grid two sides of a parallelogram have been drawn. Complete the diagram.

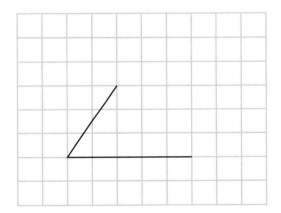

(1 mark)

 6. Complete the drawing so that it has rotational symmetry of order 4.

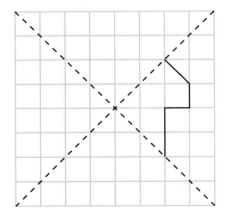

(2 marks)

(Total: _____ / 15 marks)

Congruency, Similarity and 3-D Shapes

1. **(a)** Which shape is congruent to shape A?

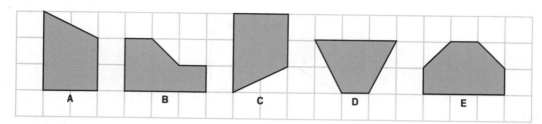

Answer: _____

(1 mark)

(b) Draw a shape that is similar to shape D. The top side has been drawn for you.

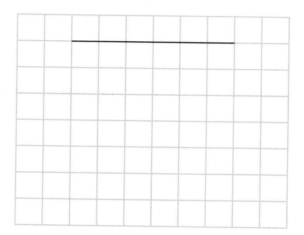

(1 mark)

2.

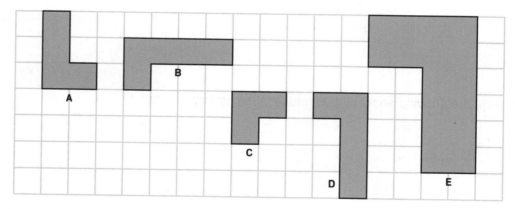

(a) Which **two** shapes are congruent?

Answer: _____

(1 mark)

(b) Which **two** shapes are similar?

Answer: _____

(1 mark)

3.

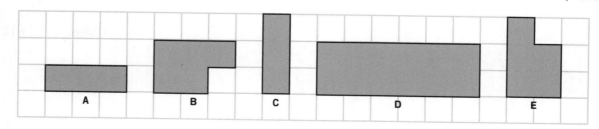

AQA GCSE Maths Foundation Exam Practice Workbook Answers

*Key: M are marks for method (e.g. **M1** means 1 mark for method); A are accuracy marks (e.g. **A1** means 1 mark for accuracy); B are independent marks that do not require method to be shown (e.g. **B2** means 2 independent marks); Q are marks for quality of written communication (e.g. **Q1** means 1 QWC mark).*

You are encouraged to show your working out, as you may be awarded marks for method even if your final answer is wrong. Full marks can be awarded where a correct answer is given without working being shown but if a question asks for working out, you must show it to gain full marks. If you use a correct method that is not shown in the mark scheme below, you would still gain full credit for it.

Basic Number Work (pages 4–5)

1. **B1 (a)** Three thousand and twenty-five
   B1 (b) 2009

2. **M1** $55 \div 4$
   A1 13.75
   B1 14 **(Mark given for rounding up)**

3. **B1 (a)** 600 **(Accept hundreds)**
   M1 (b) An attempt at multiplication, e.g. units digit 4 seen
   M1 374 or digits 561 seen
   A1 5984

4. **B1 (a)** 453
   B1 (b) 362
   B1 (c) 945
   B1 (d) 175

5. **B1 (a)** 57 and 63
   B1 (b) 63 and 25
   B1 (c) 4473

6. **B1 (a)** 29 and 41
   B1 (b) 11 and 29
   B1 (c) 55

7. **M1** 1328×15.5 or 1328×0.155
   M1 20 584 or 0.155 used
   A1 £205.84

Positive and Negative Numbers (pages 6–7)

1. **B1** $-7°C$

2. **(a)** The balance column should be completed as follows:
   B1 £428.05
   B1 £367.25
   Q1 £787.90 **(Must be correct money notation for mark)**
   B1 (b) Any valid reason, e.g. you owe the bank money or more has been taken out than paid in

3. **B1 (a)** -1
   B1 (b) -48
   B1 (c) 12

4.

3	-4	1
-2	0	2
-1	4	-3

   B2 Fully correct **(B1 for at least three correct values)**

5. **B1 (a)** $630°C$
   B1 (b) $-180°C$

6. **B1 (a)** -5 and -3
   B1 (b) 5 and -5
   M1 (c) $5 - (-5)$ **(Allow mark for attempt to use 5 and −5)**
   A1 10

Rounding (pages 8–9)

1. **M1** 40 or 300 seen or 40×300

A1 12 000

2. **M1** 100 or 5 seen or 100×5
   A1 500

3. **M1** $20 \div 2.50$ or £2.50 seen
   A1 8

4. **B1 (a)** 134.32
   B1 (b) 134.3 **(Award mark if incorrect answer in (a) is rounded correctly)**

5. **B1 (a)** 3.680 952 381…
   B1 (b) 3.7 **(Award mark if incorrect answer in (a) is rounded correctly)**

6. **B1 (a)** 1.634 013 464…
   B1 (b) 2 **(Award mark if incorrect answer in (a) is rounded correctly)**

7. **B1 (a)** 1091.082 039…
   B1 (b) 1000 **(Award mark if incorrect answer in (a) is rounded correctly)**

8. **M1** 20×30
   A1 £600

   Round the numbers to one significant figure.

9. **M1** 70×2
   A1 140 miles

   Round 68 to 70 and 1 hour 55 minutes to 2 hours.

10. **M1** $\dfrac{200 \times 50}{40}$ **(Award mark for rounding at least two of the numbers)**
    A1 250

    Round 198 to 200, 51 to 50 and 39 to 40.

11. **M1** $\dfrac{40}{10 \times 0.2}$ **(Award mark for rounding at least two of the numbers)**
    M1 $\dfrac{40}{2}$
    Q1 20 seen and Alf is correct. **(Mark given for correct conclusion)**

    Insert brackets around the denominator and work out $40 \div (10 \times 0.2) = 40 \div 2$, so the answer is about 20.

Multiples and Factors (pages 10–11)

1. **B1 (a)** 15 or 17
   B1 (b) 10 or 15
   B1 (c) 8
   B1 (d) 17

2. **M1 (a)** $2 + 12$
   A1 14
   M1 (b) 25 or 9 seen
   A1 16

3. **M1** Multiples of 12 (12, 24, 36, 48, 60, …) or multiples of 10 (10, 20, 30, 40, 50, 60, …) listed **(Up to at least 60 to gain the mark)**
   A1 60 identified as the LCM of 10 and 12
   Q1 5 packs of bread rolls and 6 packs of burgers

   For the quality of written communication mark, you must state the number of packs.

4. **M1** Multiples of 6 or multiples of 8 listed
   A1 24 or 48
   A1 24 and 48

5. **M1** Multiples of 30 listed (30, 60, 90, 120, …) **(Up to at least 120 to gain the mark)**
M1 Multiples of 40 listed (40, 80, 120, …) **(Up to at least 120 to gain the mark)**
A1 120 seconds or 2 minutes

7am is not used to answer the question but 7.02 would be accepted as the correct answer.

6. **M1** 27 or 36 seen
M1 Factor pairs of 72 seen, e.g. 2×36 or 3×24
A1 36

List multiples of 9 between 20 and 40, i.e. 27 and 36. Decide which of these is a factor of 72 ($2 \times 36 = 72$)

7. **M1 (a)** $24 = 2 \times 2 \times 2 \times 3$ or $24 = 2^3 \times 3$
or 24, 48, 72 and 36, 72… listed
A1 72
M1 (b) $60 = 2 \times 2 \times 3 \times 5$
or $2 \times 2 \times 3$
A1 12

8. **M1** Any factor pair of 96 seen (2×48, 3×32, 4×24, 6×16 or 8×12)
M1 96 as a product of three factors, e.g. $2 \times 2 \times 24$
A1 $2^5 \times 3$

Fractions (pages 12–13)

1. **B1 (a)** 9 parts shaded
M1 (b) $\frac{6}{10}$
A1 $\frac{3}{5}$

2. **M1** $\frac{5}{10} - \frac{2}{10}$
A1 $\frac{3}{10}$

3. **B2** $\frac{2}{3} \quad \frac{3}{4} \quad \frac{5}{6}$ **(B1 for equivalent fractions, e.g. $\frac{9}{12}, \frac{8}{12}, \frac{10}{12}$ or decimals 0.66…, 0.75, 0.83…)**

4. **M1** $\frac{1}{3} \times 360$ or 120 or $\frac{3}{10} \times 360$ or 108
M1 $360 - 120 - 108$
A1 132

5. **M1** $\frac{1}{4} \times 28$ or £7 or $\frac{3}{4} \times 28$
A1 £21

6. **M1** $\frac{8}{5}$
A1 $1\frac{3}{5}$

7. **M1** $\frac{1}{3} \times 18$ or 6 boys study history
A1 $\frac{6}{30}$
A1 $\frac{1}{5}$

Work out the number of boys ($30 - 12 = 18$). One-third of 18 is 6 studying history, so as a fraction of the class this is $\frac{6}{30}$ or $\frac{1}{5}$

8. **M1** $\frac{2}{3} \times 45 = 30$
M1 $\frac{3}{4} \times 44 = 33$
Q1 $\frac{3}{4}$ of 44 is bigger than $\frac{2}{3}$ of 45

$\frac{2}{3}$ of 45 is $45 \div 3 \times 2 = 30$, $\frac{3}{4}$ of 44 is $44 \div 4 \times 3 = 33$

9. **M1** $\frac{18}{30} = \frac{36}{60}$ or 0.6
M1 $\frac{13}{20} = \frac{39}{60}$ or 0.65
Q1 13 out of 20 is the better score.

You must compare using the same denominators or decimals. Any common denominator can be used.

10. **M1** $2\frac{3}{12}$ kg or $3\frac{8}{12}$ kg **(Attempt to find a common denominator gains the mark)**
A1 $2\frac{3}{12} + 3\frac{8}{12}$ **(Both must be correct to gain the mark)**
A1 $5\frac{11}{12}$ kg
Q1 Matt is not correct as $5\frac{11}{12}$ kg is less than 6 kg.

Find a common denominator in order to add fractions. For the quality of written communication mark, you must state that he is not correct.

Decimals (pages 14–15)

1. **B2** 80.9, 81.07, 81.7, 87.1, 89.0 **(B1 for four in the correct order)**

2. **B1 (a)** 8.1
B1 (b) 3.6

3. **B1 (a)** £11.09
B1 (b) £7.45

4. **B1 (a)** £1.35 (Apples)
B1 £2.30 (Loaves)
B1 £5.15 (Total)
B1 (b) £4.85 **(Award mark for correct subtraction from £10 if incorrect total in part (a))**

5. **B1 (a)** 2.5
B1 (b) 3.5
B1 (c) 0.3

6. **M1** $(3.6 + 4.9) \div 2$ or $(4.9 - 3.6) \div 2$ or 0.65
A1 4.25

7. **M1** Adds any two items correctly, e.g. £5.95 + £19.50 = £25.45
A1 Finds the correct total: £9.45 + £14.75 = £24.20
Q1 States book and gift set

For the quality of written communication mark, the items must be stated and the total worked out.

8. **M1** $5 \div 8$
A1 0.625

9. **M1** $8.4 - 3$
A1 5.4

10. **M1** $8.70 + 8.70 + 5.40 + 5.40$ or £28.20
M1 $28.20 - 22.50$
A1 £5.70

Percentages (pages 16–17)

1.

Percentage	Fraction	Decimal
25%	$\frac{1}{4}$	0.25
30%	$\frac{3}{10}$	0.3
75%	$\frac{3}{4}$	0.75

B3 Fully correct **(B1 for each correct row)**

2. **M1** $\frac{32}{100}$

   A1 $\frac{8}{25}$

3. **M1** $\frac{35}{60} \times 100$

   A1 58% or 58.3...%

4. **M1** $\frac{8}{100} \times 15\,000$ or $15\,000 \div 12$

   M1 $\frac{8}{100} \times 15\,000 \div 12$

   A1 £100

5. **M1** $\frac{20}{100} \times 350$ or £70 or 1.2×350

   M1 $\frac{30}{100} \times 560$ or £168 or 0.7×560

   A1 £420 or £392

   Q1 £420 and £392 and My TV is cheaper

   For the quality of written communication mark, you must show all working and state which is cheaper.

6. **M1** Reduction = 60 − 35 or £25

   M1 $\frac{25}{60} \times 100$

   A1 41.7%

7. **M1** $\frac{20}{100} \times 500$ or 100 grams or 1.2 seen

   M1 500 + 100 or 1.2×500

   A1 600 grams

8. **M1** $\frac{15}{100} \times 5000$ or £750 or 1.15×5000

   M1 5750 − 2000 or £3750

   M1 $\frac{18}{100} \times 3750$ or £675 or 0.82×3750

   M1 3750 − 675 or £3075 or £5075

   Q1 He has made £75 profit.

   £5000 increased by 15% is $5000 \times 1.15 = £5750$. He then has £2000 in cash and £3750 in shares. £3750 reduced by 18% is $3750 \times 0.82 = £3075$, so he now has cash and shares worth £5075.

9. **M1** $\frac{3}{16} \times 100$ or $\frac{4}{14} \times 100$

   A1 Rosie 18.75% or Jason 28.6%

   Q1 Rosie 18.75% and Jason 28.6% and Jason had the greater percentage increase.

   Percentage increase = $\dfrac{increase}{original\ amount} \times 100$, so Rosie is $\dfrac{3}{16} \times 100$ and Jason is $\dfrac{4}{14} \times 100$

Powers and Roots (pages 18–19)

1. **B1 (a)** 169
   B1 (b) 125

2. **B1 (a)** 529
   B1 (b) 704.969

3. **B1** 81

4. **B1 (a)** 11
   B1 (b) 3

5. **B1** $4^2 = 16$
   B1 $2^3 = 8$
   Q1 $4^2 = 16$ and $2^3 = 8$ and 4^2 is bigger.

   For the quality of written communication mark, you must state that 4^2 is bigger.

6. **B1 (a)** 2^9
   B1 (b) 3^4
   M1 (c) 5^3
   A1 125

7. **B1 (a)** 6^6
   B1 (b) 5^6
   B1 (c) 7

8. **B1 (a)** 196
   B1 (b) 1.96

   $1.4^2 = (14 \div 10)^2 = 14^2 \div 10^2 = 196 \div 100$

9. **B1 (a)** 2^4
   B1 (b) 2^7 **(Allow mark if power of 2 is 3 more than in part (a))**

10. **B2** $64^1 = 64$ $8^2 = 64$ $4^3 = 64$ $2^4 = 16$ **(Any one correctly worked out to gain the first mark and at least two correctly worked out to gain the second mark)**

    Q1 $64^1 = 64$ and $8^2 = 64$ and $4^3 = 64$ and $2^4 = 16$ is the odd one out

    You must show all your working and state which is the odd one out.

Ratio (pages 20–21)

1. **B1 (a)** 4 : 1
   M1 (b) 1250 g or 0.25 kg or 1250 : 250
   A1   5 : 1

2. **M1** 1 cm : 4000 m **(Knowing that 1 km = 1000 m)**
   M1 1 cm : 400 000 cm **(Knowing that 1 m = 100 cm)**
   A1 1 : 400 000

3. **M1** $60 \div 3$ or £20
   A1 £40 : £20

4. **M1** $85 \div 5$
   M1 $85 \div 5 \times 3$ or $85 \div 5 \times 2$
   A1 £51 : £34

5. **M1** $140 \div 7$
   M1 $140 \div 7 \times 2$ or $140 \div 7 \times 5$
   A1 40 grams : 100 grams

6. **M1** $63 \div 9$
   M1 $63 \div 9 \times 2$ or $63 \div 9 \times 3$ or $63 \div 9 \times 4$
   A1 14 grams : 21 grams : 28 grams

7. **M1** $35 \div 7$
   M1 $35 \div 7 \times 2$ or 10 or $35 \div 7 \times 5$ or 25 or $35 \div 7 \times 3$
   A1 £15

8. **M1** $750 \div 6$
   M1 $750 \div 6 \times 5$
   A1 625 ml

9. **M1** $100\% \div 5 \times 4$ or $\frac{4}{5}$ seen
   A1 80%

   All the mortar is 100%. Dividing 100% in the ratio 4 : 1 gives 80% : 20%

10. **M1** $\frac{2}{3} \times 120$ or £80

    M1 $80 \div 8$ or £10 or 10×5
    A1 £50

    Two-thirds of £120 = £80. So £80 is shared in the ratio 3 : 5, giving £30 : £50, so £50 is the larger share.

11. **M1** $180 \div 9$
    M1 $180 \div 9 \times 7$ or $180 \div 9 \times 2$
    A1 140 or 40
    M1 $140 \times 38 + 40 \times 54$
    A1 £7480

    Dividing 180 in the ratio 7 : 2 gives 140 : 40, so 140 passengers travel standard class and 40 passengers travel first class. $140 \times 38 + 40 \times 54 = £7480$

Proportion (pages 22–23)

1. **B1** 120 grams butter / flour / caster sugar
   B1 80 grams jam
   B1 60 ml cream
   B1 2 eggs

2. **M1** Butter will make 15 biscuits or $\frac{75}{100} \times 20$

   M1 Flour will make 12 biscuits or $\frac{150}{250} \times 20$

   Q1 12 biscuits

   For the quality of written communication mark, both answers must be seen and the correct answer given.

3. **M1** $120 \div 2.5$
   A1 48 mph

4. **M1 (a)** 500×1.55
   A1 $775
   M1 (b) $900 \div 1.55$
   A1 £580.65 **(Allow any answer in the range £580 to £581)**

5. **M1** £1.72 ÷ 4 or £1.18 ÷ 2 or £5.40 ÷ 12 **(Any comparison for at least two equal quantities to gain the mark)**
   A1 43p or 59p or 45p **(Any comparison for three equal quantities to gain the mark)**
   Q1 Three correct values for comparison, e.g. 43p and 59p and 45p and pack of 4 stated

   For the quality of written communication mark, all three packs must be compared and the correct answer given.

6. **M1** £1.46 ÷ 6 or £1.98 ÷ 10 **(Any comparison of equal quantities to gain the mark)**
   A1 £0.243… or £0.198 or 24p or 19.8p or 20p **(Any comparison for two equal quantities to gain the mark)**
   Q1 Two correct values for comparison, e.g. 24.3p or 24p and 19.8p or 20p and 10 eggs stated

   For the quality of written communication mark to be awarded, both packs must be compared and the correct answer given.

Basic Algebra (pages 24–25)

1. **B1 (a)** $x + 5$ or $5 + x$
   B1 (b) $\frac{1}{3}y$ or $\frac{y}{3}$

2. **M1 (a)** $15 \div 5 \times 8$ or 3×8
   A1 24 km
   M1 (b) $60 \div 8 \times 5$
   A1 37.5 miles

3. **B1 (a)** 9am
   B1 (b) 4.45am

4. **B1 (a)** $7x$
   B2 (b) $-7x + 9y$ **(B1 for $-7x$; B1 for $9y$)**

5. **B1 (a)** Equation
   B1 (b) Formula
   B1 (c) Expression

6. **M1 (a)** $2 \times 5 - 3 \times -2$ or $10 + 6$
   A1 16
   M1 (b) $(5)^2 - (-2)^2$
   M1 $25 - 4$
   A1 21

7. **M1** $-2x + 12y$ or $a = -2$ or $b = 12$
   A1 $a = -2$ and $b = 12$

   Simplify the expression first and then write down the values of a and b.

8. **M1** If n is even $5n$ is even, so $5n + 3$ is even + odd = odd
   If n is odd $5n$ is odd, so $5n + 3$ is odd + odd = even
   A1 $5n + 3$ could be either odd or even.

   You must consider both when n is odd and when n is even.

9. **B1 (a)** Odd

   Odd + even = odd

   B1 (b) Even

   Odd × even = even

   B1 (c) Even

   Even + even = even

10. **M1** $y + 6 = 5x$ or $\frac{y}{5} = x - \frac{6}{5}$

    A1 $x = \frac{y + 6}{5}$ or $x = \frac{y}{5} + \frac{6}{5}$

Working with Brackets & Trial and Improvement (pages 26–27)

1. **B1** $3x - 18$

2. **B1** $x^2 + 4x$

3. **M1** $2x - 2 + 3x + 9$ **(Allow one error)**
   A1 $5x + 7$

4. **M1** $14x + 21 - 4x + 6$ **(Allow one error)**
   A1 $10x + 27$

5. **B1** $5(x - 2)$

6. **B2** $3x(x + 2)$ **(B1 for $3(x^2 + 2x)$ or $x(3x + 6)$)**

7. **B1** $2(4x + 5)$

8. **B2** $5y(x - 4y)$ **(B1 for $5(xy - 4y^2)$ or $y(5x - 20y)$)**

9. **B1** Valid explanation, e.g. it should be $4x(x + 2y)$

   You should explain that it is not fully factorised.

10. **M1** Tests any value between 2 and 3
    M1 Works out that solution is between $x = 2.5$ and $x = 2.6$, e.g. $2.5 \to 18.125$ (too small), $2.6 \to 20.176$ (too big)
    M1 Tests a value between 2.5 and 2.6, e.g. $x = 2.55 \to 19.131\ldots$ (too small)
    A1 $x = 2.6$

11. **M1** Tests any whole number value, e.g. $1 \to -2$, $2 \to 2$, $3 \to 18$, $4 \to 52$
    M1 Works out that solution is between $x = 3$ and $x = 4$, e.g. $3 \to 18$ (too small), $4 \to 52$ (too big)
    M1 Works out that solution is between $x = 3.4$ and $x = 3.5$, e.g. $3.4 \to 29.104$ (too small), $3.5 \to 32.375$ (too big)
    A1 Tests a value between 3.4 and 3.5 and gives $x = 3.4$ (1 d.p.), e.g. $3.45 \to 30.71$ (too big)

Linear Equations (pages 28–29)

1. **B1 (a)** $x = 22$
   B1 (b) $x = 3$

2. **M1 (a)** $7x = 23 + 5$ or $7x = 28$
   A1 $x = 4$
   M1 (b) $3x - x = 5 - 4$ or $2x = 1$
   A1 $x = \frac{1}{2}$

3. **M1 (a)** $5x - 2x = -15 - 6$ or $3x = -21$
   A1 $x = -7$
   M1 (b) $8x - 4 = 28$ or $2x - 1 = 7$
   M1 $8x = 28 + 4$ or $8x = 32$ or $2x = 8$
   A1 $x = 4$

4. **M1** $\frac{x}{2} = 9 - 5$ or $\frac{x}{2} = 4$
   A1 $x = 8$

5. **B1** $4x - 7 = 3x + 5$
   M1 $4x - 3x = 5 + 7$
   A1 $x = 12$

   Let the number they are thinking of be x. Now set up and solve an equation.

6.   **M1** Son's age now is $x - 28$
       M1 In five years my age is $x + 5$, son's age is $x - 28 + 5$ or $x - 23$
       M1 $x + 5 = 2(x - 23)$
       M1 $x + 5 = 2x - 46$
       A1 $x = 51$

> *Write down in terms of x the ages now and in five years. Then set up and solve an equation.*

7.   **M1** $3x + 2x + x + 60° = 180°$
       M1 $6x + 60° = 180°$ or $6x = 180° - 60°$
       A1 $x = 20°$
       Q1 Largest angle is $x + 60° = 80°$

> *Remember to check that you have worked out the largest angle. The angles are 60°, 40° and 80°.*

Patterns and Sequences (pages 30–31)

1.   **B1 (a)**

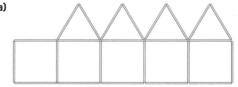

       B1 (b) 29
       M1 (c) 49 seen or 10th pattern
       A1   1 stick left over

2.   **B1 (a)** 33
       B1   37 **(Award mark if 4 more than the first answer)**
       B1 (b) Add 4

3.   **B1 (a)** 2
       B1   −2 **(Award mark if 4 less than the first answer)**
       B1 (b) Subtract 4

4.   **B2 (a)** $3n + 4$ **(B1 for $3n + c$ where c is any value)**
       B1 (b) Valid explanation, e.g. $3n + 4 = 152$ gives $3n = 148$, $n = 49.3…$ so not a whole number, or sequence goes …$n = 49 \rightarrow 151$, $n = 50 \rightarrow 154$…

> *Remember that for a term to be in the sequence, n must be a whole number.*

5.   **M1 (a)** $5 \times 6 - 3$ or $30 - 3$
       A1   27
       B1 (b) No and valid explanation, e.g. $5n - 3 = 85$ gives $5n = 88$, $n = 17.6$ so not a whole number, or sequence goes 82, 87

6.   **M1** $1 + 2 + 3 + 4 + 5 + 6 + 7 = 28$
       A1 7 tins in bottom layer

> *Keep adding on consecutive numbers until you reach 28, i.e. $1 + 2 = 3$, $1 + 2 + 3 = 6$, and so on.*

7.   **M1 (a)** 2, 4, 6 or states goes up in 2s
       A1 $2n$
       M1 (b) 4, 7, 10 or states goes up in 3s or $3n$
       A1 $3n + 1$

> *Always write down the number of circles in the pattern first.*

Straight Line Graphs (pages 32–33)

1.   **B1 (a)** −7 and 2
       (b)

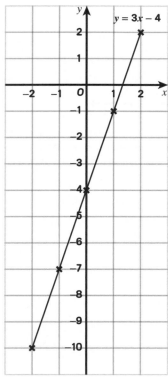

       B1 At least two correct points plotted
       B1 Straight line through the points **(Line must be ruled)**

2.

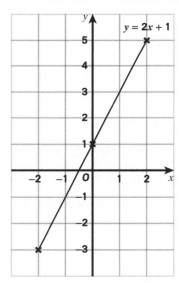

       B1 At least one correct point calculated or plotted
       B1 Two correct points calculated or plotted
       B1 Straight line through the points **(Line must be ruled)**

3.

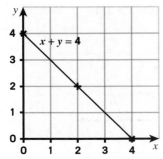

B1 At least one correct point calculated or plotted
B1 Two correct points calculated or plotted
B1 Straight line through the points **(Line must be ruled)**

4.

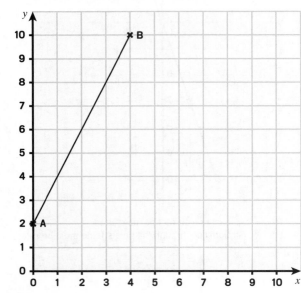

B2 (a) Points plotted correctly **(B1 for each)**
B1 (b) Straight line between the points **(Line must be ruled)**
M1 (c) Triangle drawn to work out gradient or gradient $= \dfrac{10-2}{4-0}$
A1 Gradient = 2

> Remember that gradient $= \dfrac{\text{distance up the triangle}}{\text{distance across the triangle}}$ or
> $\dfrac{\text{difference of } y \text{-coordinates}}{\text{difference of } x \text{-coordinates}}$

Linear Inequalities and Quadratic Graphs (pages 34–35)

1. M1 (a) $2x < 7 - 1$ or $2x < 6$
   A1 $x < 3$

   (b)

   B2 Fully correct **(B1 for either a closed circle at 2 or an open circle at 5)**

> Remember to use a solid circle to include a number and an open circle if the number is not included.

2. B1 (a) $x < 1$
   M1 (b) $4x \leqslant 17 + 3$ or $4x \leqslant 20$
   A1 $x \leqslant 5$

3. B1 (a) $x \leqslant 3$
   B2 (b) 0, 1, 2 **(B1 for two correct values, e.g. 1, 2 or −1, 0, 1)**

4. B1 (a) Cost of 3 light bulbs is £3x and this is less than or equal to £3.50
   B1 (b) Cost of 4 light bulbs is £4x and this is more than £3.50
   M1 (c) £3.50 ÷ 3 or 1.166 666…
   A1 £1.16

> You need to round down to a sensible money value.

5. (a)

x	−2	−1	0	1	2
y	6	**3**	**2**	3	**6**

B2 All values correct **(B1 for one or two correct values)**

(b)

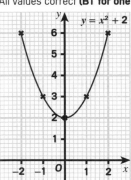

B1 Points plotted
B1 Smooth curve through all the points

6. (a)

x	−1	0	1	2	3	4
y	3	**0**	−1	**0**	3	8

B2 All values correct **(B1 for one or two correct values)**

(b)

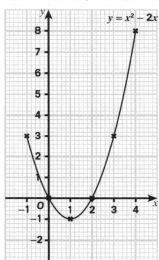

B1 Points plotted
B1 Smooth curve through all the points

Real-life Graphs (pages 36–37)

1. **B1 (a)**

Kilograms	0	10	20
Pounds	0	**22**	**44**

(b)

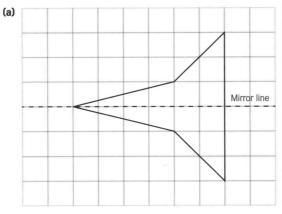

B1   Two correct points plotted
B1   Straight line through the points **(Line must be ruled)**
B1 (c) 31 pounds **(Allow 30 pounds to 32 pounds)**
M1 (d) Reads off graph at either 18 kg or 37 pounds
A1   39 pounds to 40 pounds or 16 kg to 17 kg
Q1   18 kg is greater

For the quality of written communication mark, the decision must be supported by a correct conversion.

2. **B1 (a)** 24 cm to 26 cm
   M1 (b) 5×12 or 60
   M1 $6 \times$ answer to part **(a)**, e.g. 6×25
   A1   150 cm

   Convert 5 feet into inches, then convert from inches to centimetres.

3. **B1 (a)** 40 miles
   B1 (b) 2 hours

4. **B1 (a)** Usain, Carl, Ben
   B3 (b) Any three correct facts apart from order in part **(a)**
   repeated, e.g. Usain led all the way; Carl overtook Ben;
   Carl was last for the first part of the race; Usain won in
   54 seconds; Carl finished in 65 seconds; Ben finished
   in 74 seconds. **(B1 for each)**

Symmetry and Shapes (pages 38–39)

1. **(a)**

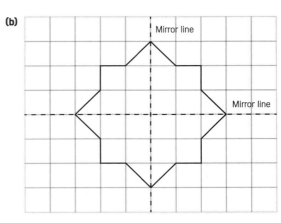

2. **(b)**

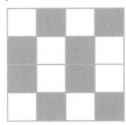

B2   Fully correct **(B1 for line symmetry about one mirror line)**

2. **B1** Shape A: Order 5
   B1 Shape B: Order 4
   B1 Shape C: Order 2

3. **(a)**

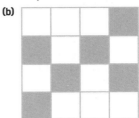

B2   Fully correct **(B1 for one square correct)**

(b)

B2   Fully correct **(B1 for one square correct)**

4. **B1 (a)** Right-angled
   B1 (b) Trapezium

5.

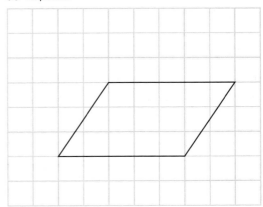

B1 Fully correct

B1 Fully correct

6.

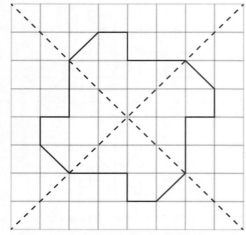

B2 Fully correct **(B1 for one quarter correct)**

Congruency, Similarity and 3-D Shapes (pages 40–41)

1. **B1 (a)** C
   (b)

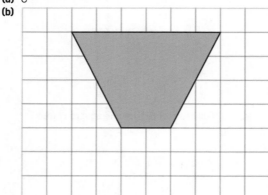

   B1 Fully correct

2. **B1 (a)** B and D
   B1 (b) A and E

3. **B1 (a)** E
   B1 (b) A and C
   B1 (c) A and D or C and D

4. Any suitable answer, e.g.

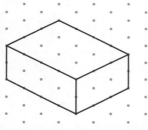

   B2 Fully correct **(B1 for any cuboid or for at least one face correct)**

5.

	Faces	Edges	Vertices
Cuboid	6	12	8
Square-based Pyramid	5	8	5

   B4 Fully correct **(B1 for each correct entry)**

6. **B1 (a)** 3 cm
   M1 (b) Angle $A = 180° - 90° - 37°$
   A1 Angle $A = 53°$

Angles and Parallel Lines (pages 42–43)

1. **B1 (a)** 105°
   B1 (b) (i) 130°
   B1 (ii) Corresponding angles

   Make sure that you use the correct words. Do not call them 'F' angles.

2. **B1 (a)** 47°
   M1 (b) Angle $CED = 180° - 112°$ or angle $CED = 68°$
   M1 $y = 180° - 47° - 68°$
   A1 $y = 65°$

   There are many ways to work out this answer. Fill in the angles you know on the diagram.

3. **M1** $x = 180° - 75° - 86°$
   A1 $x = 19°$

4. **M1 (a)** $x = 180° - 70°$
   A1 $x = 110°$
   M1 (b) Angle $BAC = 180° - 25° - 110° = 45°$
   M1 Angle $ACB = (180° - 45°) \div 2 = 67.5°$
   M1 $y = 180° - 70° - 67.5°$
   A1 $y = 42.5°$

   Remember the properties of an isosceles triangle.

5. **M1 (a)** $x + 40° + x - 30° = 180°$
   M1 $2x + 10° = 180°$
   M1 $2x = 180° - 10°$ or $2x = 170°$
   A1 $x = 85°$

   Set up an equation in terms of x. Allied angles add up to 180°.

   M1 (b) $y = x + 40°$ or $y = 85° + 40°$
   A1 $y = 125°$

Angles of Polygons (pages 44–45)

1. **M1 (a)** $x = 360° - 110° - 40° - 80°$
   A1 $x = 130°$
   B1 (b) Angles on a straight line add up to 180° and angles in a quadrilateral add up to 360°.

2. **M1 (a)** $3x + 2x + 100° + x + 20°$ or using 360°
   A1 $3x + 2x + 100° + x + 20° = 360°$
   M1 (b) $6x + 120° = 360°$ or $6x = 240°$
   A1 $x = 40°$ **(Full marks can be gained from an incorrect but reasonable value followed through from (a))**

3. **M1 (a)** $180° - 150°$
   A1 30°
   M1 (b) $360° \div 30°$
   A1 12 sides

4. **M1** Working out the exterior angle of the hexagon: $360° \div 6$
   M1 60° or $180° - 60°$ or 120° (interior angle in hexagon)
   M1 $360° - 120° - 90° - 90°$
   A1 60°

   Work out the interior angle of the hexagon first, then use angles at a point add up to 360°.

5. **M1** Working out an exterior angle: $360° \div 6$ or $360° \div 8$
   A1 60° or 45°
   M1 $60° + 45°$
   A1 105°

   The two exterior angles add up to make the angle marked x.

Perimeter and Area (pages 46–47)

1. **B1** **(a)** Area of shape A = 9 cm²
   B1   Area of shape B = 8 cm²
   Q1   Shape A has the greater area.

   Remember to state which area is greater for the final mark.

   B1 **(b)** Perimeter of shape A = 16 cm
   B1   Perimeter of shape B = 14 cm
   Q1   Shape A has the greater perimeter.

   Remember to state which perimeter is greater for the final mark.

2. **M1** Attempt to count squares
   A1 Answer in range 12 cm² to 16 cm²

3. **B2** **(a)** Correct net with six faces, e.g.

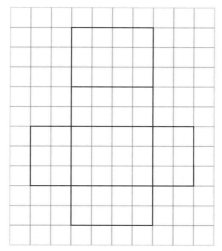

   (B1 for five correct faces or correct net but wrong size)
   M1 **(b)** 4×3 or 4×2 or 3×2
   M1 $(4 \times 3 + 4 \times 2 + 3 \times 2) \times 2$
   A1   52 cm²

4.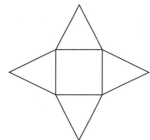

   B1 Fully correct sketch

Areas of Triangles and Quadrilaterals (pages 48–49)

1. **M1** $\frac{1}{2} \times 10 \times 6$
   A1 30 cm²

2. **M1** $\frac{1}{2} \times (4 + 8) \times 5$
   A1 30 cm²

3. **M1** 8×4
   A1 32 cm²

4. **M1** $30 - 4$ or 26 and $20 - 4$ or 16 seen
   M1 $30 \times 20 - 26 \times 16$
   A1 184 cm²

   Subtract the area of the small rectangle from the area of the large rectangle.

5. **M1** Triangle *AMD* is one-quarter of the rectangle
   M1 Triangle *DCN* is one-quarter of the rectangle
   A1 Fraction left = $1 - \frac{1}{4} - \frac{1}{4} = \frac{1}{2}$

   Work out what fraction of the rectangle the triangles cover.

6. **M1** $\frac{1}{2} \times 12 \times 4$ or 24
   M1 $\frac{1}{2} \times 8 \times h = 24$
   A1 $h = 6$ cm

   Work out the area of the first triangle and use your answer in the second triangle.

7. **M1** Height of rectangle = 6 cm or height of triangle = 3 cm
   M1 10×6 or $\frac{1}{2} \times 10 \times 3$
   M1 $60 + 15$
   A1 75 cm²

   Divide 9 cm in the ratio 2 : 1 to find the height of the rectangle and the height of the triangle.

Circumference and Area of Circles (pages 50–51)

1. **M1** $2 \times \pi \times 10$
   A1 20π cm or $\pi \times 20$ cm

2. **M1** $\pi \times 6 \times 6$
   A1 113 cm²

3. **M1** $\pi \times 7 \times 7$
   A1 49π cm²

4. **M1** $(2 \times \pi \times 5.1) \div 2$ or $\pi \times 5.1$
   M1 $16.0 + 5.1 + 5.1$ **(Use of an incorrect value in place of 16.0 would still get the mark)**
   A1 26.2 cm

5. **M1** $\pi \times 5 \times 5$
   M1 $\pi \times 5 \times 5 \div 4$
   A1 19.6 cm²

6. **M1** $\pi \times 6 \times 6$ or $\pi \times 5 \times 5$
   M1 $\pi \times 6 \times 6 - \pi \times 5 \times 5$ or $36\pi - 25\pi$
   A1 Answer in range 34.5 m² to 34.6 m²

   Subtract the area of the small circle from the area of the large circle.

7. **M1** $2 \times \pi \times 30$ or $\pi \times 60$
   M1 $\pi \times 60 \times 1000$ (distance to cover 1000 revolutions)
   M1 $\pi \times 60 \times 1000 \div 100$
   A1 1884 m or 1885 m

   Remember that 1 metre = 100 centimetres

Plan and Elevation (pages 52–53)

1. **B1** **(a)**

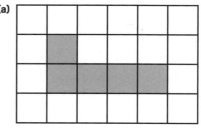

   B1 **(b)**

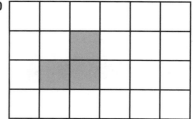

2.

M1 Attempt at drawing a square-based pyramid or statement that it is a square-based pyramid

A1 Clear drawing of square-based pyramid showing at least two faces

If you have difficulty sketching the shape then write down its name.

3. Any suitable answer, e.g.

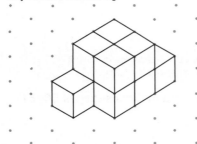

B2 Fully correct **(B1 for at least one view correct)**

Practice drawing one cube first. Try not to draw the hidden edges.

4.

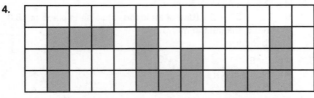

Plan View   Front Elevation   Side Elevation

B3 Fully correct **(B1 for each view, accept elevations in either order)**

Volumes of Prisms (pages 54–55)

1. **M1** Volume of cuboid: $6 \times 3 \times 2$
A1 36 cm³

2. **M1 (a)** Area of triangle: $\frac{1}{2} \times 8 \times 6$
A1 24 cm²

M1 (b) Volume of prism: $\frac{1}{2} \times 8 \times 6 \times 9$ or 24×9
A1 216 cm³

3. **M1** Volume of prism: 16×12
A1 192 cm³

4. **M1** Area of the trapezium: $\frac{1}{2} \times (3 + 1.6) \times 2$

M1 Volume of prism: $\frac{1}{2} \times (3 + 1.6) \times 2 \times 4$ or the area $\times 4$
A1 18.4 m³

5. **M1** $\pi \times 5.6^2 \times 3.1$
A1 Answer in range 305 cm³ to 306 cm³

6. **M1 (a)** Area of one rectangle: 0.5×0.1
M1 Area of cross-section: 0.05×2 or 0.1
M1 Volume of girder: 0.1×20
A1 2 m³
M1 (b) $15 \div 2$
A1 7.5
Q1 7 **(Rounding down)**

Remember to give a whole number of girders for the final mark.

Pythagoras' Theorem (pages 56–57)

1. **M1** $6^2 + 8^2$ or $36 + 64$ or 100
M1 $\sqrt{6^2 + 8^2}$ or $\sqrt{36 + 64}$ or $\sqrt{100}$
A1 10 cm

2. **M1** $9.4^2 - 6.2^2$ or $88.36 - 38.44$ or 49.92
M1 $\sqrt{9.4^2 - 6.2^2}$ or $\sqrt{88.36 - 38.44}$ or $\sqrt{49.92}$
A1 7.065… cm
B1 7.1 cm **(Correct rounding of your answer)**

3. **M1** $8.4^2 + 5.7^2$ or $70.56 + 32.49$ or 103.05
M1 $\sqrt{8.4^2 + 5.7^2}$ or $\sqrt{70.56 + 32.49}$ or $\sqrt{103.05}$
A1 10.15… cm
B1 10.2 cm **(Correct rounding of your answer)**

4. **M1** $22 - 13$ or 9
M1 $9^2 + 10^2$ or $81 + 100$ or 181
M1 $\sqrt{9^2 + 10^2}$ or $\sqrt{81 + 100}$ or $\sqrt{181}$
A1 13.45… m or 13.5 m

Work out the distance from the gate to the other corner of the field.

5. **M1** $5^2 - 4.8^2$ or $25 - 23.04$ or 1.96
M1 $\sqrt{5^2 - 4.8^2}$ or $\sqrt{25 - 23.04}$ or $\sqrt{1.96}$
A1 1.4 m

6. **M1** $4^2 + 7.5^2$ or $16 + 56.25$ or 72.25
M1 $\sqrt{4^2 + 7.5^2}$ or $\sqrt{16 + 56.25}$ or $\sqrt{72.25}$
A1 8.5 km
M1 $4 + 7.5 + 8.5$ or 20 km
A1 20 km $\div$ 10 km/h = 2 hours

Work out the distance back to port, then the total distance covered. Remember to work out the time taken:
$$\text{Time taken} = \frac{\text{distance}}{\text{speed}}$$

Transformations (pages 58–59)

1. **(a)**

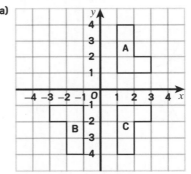

B2 Correct reflection **(B1 for a reflection in the y-axis)**
B1 (b) Rotation
B1 180°
B1 About the origin or about (0, 0)

2.

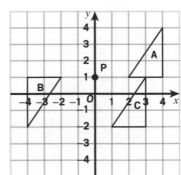

B2 (a) Fully correct **(B1 for rotation 180° in wrong position)**
B1 (b) Fully correct

3.

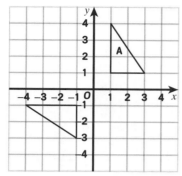

B2 Fully correct **(B1 for any reflection)**

4.

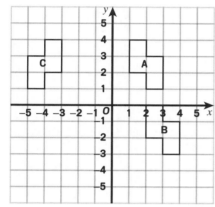

B2 **(a)** Fully correct **(B1 for correct translation in one direction)**
B2 **(b)** Fully correct **(B1 for any reflection)**

5.

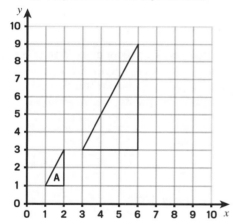

B3 Fully correct **(B2 for an enlargement scale factor 3; B1 for any enlargement, e.g. scale factor 2)**

6.

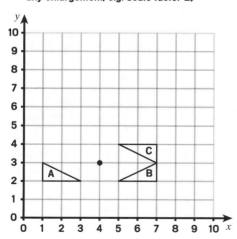

B3 Rotation, 180° about (4, 3) **(B1 for each correct statement or award B1 for each correct drawing on the diagram)**

Use the grid to draw triangles B and C.

Basic Measures (pages 60–61)

1. **B1** **(a)** 8.6 cm **(Allow answer from 8.5 cm to 8.7 cm inclusive)**
   B1 **(b)** 127° **(Allow answer from 125° to 129° inclusive)**
2. **B1** 160 ml
3. **B1** **(a)** 4 mph
   B1 **(b)** $\frac{3}{8}$
4. **B1** **(a)** $3\frac{1}{2}$ pints
   B1 **(b)** Answer in range 0.5 to 0.6 litres
5. **B1** **(a)** 25° **(Allow 23° to 27°)**
   M1 **(b)** 360° − 25°
   A1 335° **(Allow 333° to 337°. Full marks can be obtained for correctly working out 360° minus the answer to part (a))**
6. **B1** **(a)** 11 minutes
   M1 **(b)** Need to catch 1108 **(Allow attempt to subtract 15 minutes from 1108)**
   A1 1053

Conversion and Estimation (pages 62–63)

1. **B1** **(a)** Metres
   B1 **(b)** Kilograms
   B1 **(c)** Litres
2. **M1** **(a)** 700 × 1.58
   A1 $1106
   M1 **(b)** 230 ÷ 1.75 or £131.43
   A1 £131
3. **B1** **(a)** 5 miles is approximately 8 kilometres.
   M1 **(b)** 60 ÷ 5 × 8 or 8 × 12
   A1 96 km
4. **B2** **(a)** 1 kilogram is approximately 2.2 pounds.
   1 inch is approximately 2.5 centimetres.
   10 miles is approximately 16 kilometres.
   (B1 for one or two correct)
   M1 **(b)** 90 ÷ 4.5
   A1 20 gallons
5. **B1** Height of man will be approximately 1.8 m **(Allow any height between 1.5 m and 2.2 m)**
   M1 2 × height, e.g. 2 × 1.8
   A1 3.6 m **(Allow answer between 3 m and 4.4 m)**

Constructions (pages 64–65)

1. **B2** Fully correct triangle with construction arcs for at least two sides **(B1 for any correct length drawn to within 1 mm)**
2. **M1** Angle of 47° drawn **(Allow 45° to 49°)**
   A1 Fully correct triangle **(Must see construction arc for AB and AC)**
3.

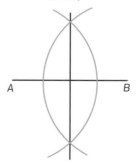

   M1 Equal arcs from A and B which intersect
   A1 Fully correct construction with perpendicular drawn

4. **B2** Fully correct triangle **(B1 for *AB* 7.5 cm to within 1 mm or at least one correct angle drawn to within 2°)**

5.

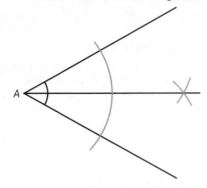

M1 Arc from vertex through both lines
A1 Fully correct construction **(Must see all construction arcs)**

6. **B1** **(a)** Side 6 cm long drawn **(Allow 5.9 cm to 6.1 cm)**
B1 Angle 40° measured **(Allow angles from 38° to 42°)**
B1 Fully correct triangle
B1 **(b)** Answer in range 3.9 cm to 4.3 cm

7.

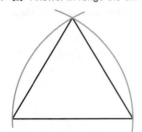

M1 Equal arcs with radius same length as line
A1 Triangle drawn with arcs seen

Bearings and Loci (pages 66–67)

1. **B1** **(a)** $x = 135°$ **(Allow any answer from 133° to 137°)**
M1 **(b)** 4.5×20 km **(Allow 4.4 to 4.6 cm for the measurement)**
A1 90 km **(Allow any answer from 88 to 92 km)**
M1 **(c)** $180° + 135°$ **(Allow 180° + answer to part (a))**
A1 315° **(Allow any answer that is 180° + answer to part (a))**

2. **B1** **(a)** Arc drawn radius 3 cm from A **(Allow 2.9 cm to 3.1 cm)**
B1 Bearing of 050° drawn at A (with B marked) **(Allow angle 048° to 052°)**
B1 Arc drawn radius 2 cm from A **(Allow 2.9 cm to 3.1 cm)**
B1 Bearing of 340° drawn at A (with C marked) **(Allow angle 338° to 342°)**
M1 **(b)** Line BC measured and length multiplied by 4 **(BC measures 3 cm if correct)**
A1 12 km

3.

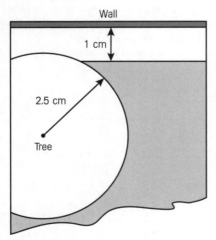

B1 Circle radius 2.5 cm from tree **(Allow from 2.4 cm to 2.6 cm)**
B1 Line 1 cm from wall **(Allow 0.9 cm to 1.1 cm)**
B1 Fully correct with shading

4.

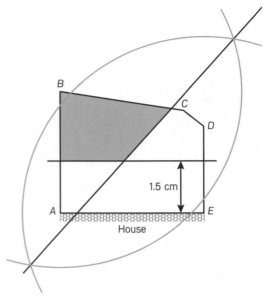

M1 Intersecting equal arcs from *B* and *E*
A1 Perpendicular bisector drawn through points of intersection
B1 Line drawn 1.5 cm from house **(Allow 1.4 cm to 1.6 cm)**
B1 Fully correct with shading

5.

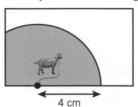

B2 Arc drawn from post with radius 4 cm **(B1 for any arc drawn from post)**

Handling Data Cycle and Questionnaires (pages 68–69)

1. **B1** Missing values, e.g. cannot tick 0 or cannot tick 8
B1 Overlapping values, e.g. 5 is in two categories

2. **B1** Suitable question, e.g. How many people are in your immediate family including you?
B1 Response section with no missing values and no overlapping values, e.g.

1 ☐   2 ☐   3 ☐   4 ☐   More than 4 ☐

3. **B1** **(a)** Question too vague / not specific enough
B1 Overlapping value of £10
B1 **(b)** Suitable question, e.g. How much did you spend on Christmas presents on average?
B1 Response section with no overlaps and no gaps, e.g.

Less than £5 ☐   £5 to £10 ☐   More than £10 ☐

B1 **(c)** Valid reason, e.g. biased towards children
B1 A different valid reason, e.g. biased towards people buying toys

4. **B1** **(a)** Cannot answer 'poor'
B1 **(b)** Suitable question with a time frame, e.g. How many times each month do you use the shop?
B1 Suitable response section with no missing values and no overlapping values, e.g.

0 ☐   1 to 2 ☐   3 to 4 ☐   More than 4 ☐

5. **B1** Collect data for different months, e.g. from the Internet
B1 Represent the data using charts or diagrams or work out the mean monthly temperature
Q1 Interpret the results and make a conclusion, e.g. compare the mean temperatures

For full marks you must refer to the context.

6. **B1** Collect data for girls and boys in year 9, e.g. from the results of a mathematics test
B1 Represent the data using charts or diagrams or work out the mean mark for girls and for boys
Q1 Interpret the results and make a conclusion, e.g. compare the mean marks

For full marks you must refer to the context.

Averages and Range (pages 70–71)

1. **B1** **(a)** Mode = 1
M1 **(b)** Sorting numbers into order: 0, 1, 1, 1, 1, 2, 2, 3, 3, 4
A1 Median = 1.5
B1 **(c)** New median = 2
Q1 States that median will increase

For the final mark, the median must be compared with the original median.

2.

Number of Eggs, x	Number of Hens, f	$f \times x$
0	2	0
1	4	4
2	5	10
3	6	18
4	13	52
	Total = 30	Total = 84

M1 Working out $f \times x$, i.e. 0, 4, 10, 18, 52
M1 Working out the total ÷ 30, i.e. 84 ÷ 30
A1 2.8 **(Accept 3 if working shown)**

3.

Time Taken, t (minutes)	Frequency, f	Mid-values, t (minutes)	$f \times t$
$15 < t \leqslant 20$	4	17.5	70
$20 < t \leqslant 25$	10	22.5	225
$25 < t \leqslant 30$	6	27.5	165
	Total = 20		Total = 460

B1 Using mid-values, i.e. 17.5, 22.5, 27.5
M1 Working out $f \times t$, i.e. 70, 225, 165
M1 Working out the total ÷ 20, i.e. 460 ÷ 20
A1 23 minutes

4. **B1** **(a)** $1.6 < h \leqslant 1.8$
B1 **(b)** $1.6 < h \leqslant 1.8$
Q1 **(c)** 19 students above 1.6 metres, of which 6 are above 1.8 metres, or distribution skewed so mean must be above 1.6 metres

Look at the shape of the distribution.

5. **B1** 5 numbers that have a total of 50
B1 5 numbers with a range of 10, e.g. 5, 9, 10, 11, 15

If 5 numbers have a mean of 10, the total must equal 50.

Collecting and Sorting Data (pages 72–73)

1. **B1** **(a)** Biased sample as it is asking people at a travel agent about holidays

(b)

Number of Holidays	Tally	Frequency
1	ǀǀǀǀ ǀǀǀǀ	10
2	ǀǀǀǀ ǀ	6
3	ǀǀǀ	3
4	ǀ	1

B1 Correct tallies
B1 Correct frequencies for their tallies

2. **B1** **(a)** 37
B1 **(b)** 49 − 21 = 28
B1 **(c)** Comment comparing the medians, e.g. on average the students did better in geography
B1 Comment comparing the ranges, e.g. the history marks are less spread out

It is not enough to simply state the medians and ranges; you have to compare the results.

3.

0	8 9
1	3 4 5 8 8 9
2	1 1 4

Key: 1 | 3 represents an age of 13

B1 Suitable key
B2 Leaves 8 9

3 4 5 8 8 9

1 1 4

(B1 for one error or unordered)
Q1 Logical organised working

4. **M1** **(a)** (81 + 22) − (43 + 24) or 103 − 67
A1 36
M1 **(b)** $\dfrac{22}{43 + 81 + 24 + 22}$
A1 $= \dfrac{22}{170}$ or $\dfrac{11}{85}$

5.

	Soaps	Comedies	Cartoons	Total
Girls	3	5	2	10
Boys	1	5	14	20
Total	4	10	16	30

B4 Fully correct (all 9 entries) **(B3 for 7 or 8 correct; B2 for 4, 5 or 6 correct; B1 for 1, 2 or 3 correct)**

Representing Data (pages 74–75)

1. Key: ⊗ represents **6** students

B2 Fully correct pictogram (all four days correct) **(B1 for at least one day correct)**
B1 Correct key

2. **B1** **(a)** 8
B1 **(b)** 18

3.

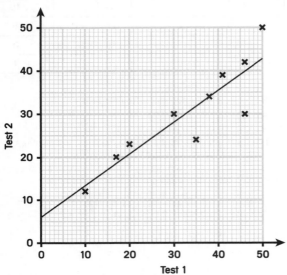

B2 **(a)** All points plotted correctly **(B1 for 7, 8 or 9 points plotted correctly)**
B1 **(b)** Straight line through the points **(There are a considerable number of suitable lines that could be drawn)**
B1 **(c)** Positive correlation
M1 **(d)** Reading off at 25
A1 Test 2 score = 24 **(Answers may vary depending on line drawn)**

4. **(a)**

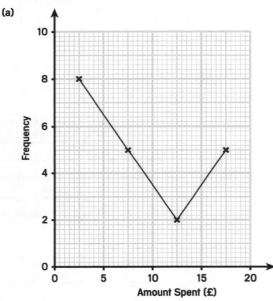

B1 Midpoints used, i.e. 2.5, 7.5, 12.5, 17.5
B1 Correct heights plotted, i.e. 8, 5, 2, 5
B1 Points joined with straight lines **(No mark if there is a line segment joining the first point directly to the last)**

(b)

Amount Spent, £A	Frequency, f	Midpoint, m	$f \times m$
$0 < A \leqslant 5$	8	2.5	20
$5 < A \leqslant 10$	5	7.5	37.5
$10 < A \leqslant 15$	2	12.5	25
$15 < A \leqslant 20$	5	17.5	87.5
	Total = 20		Total = 170

B1 Using mid-values, i.e. 2.5, 7.5, 12.5, 17.5
M1 Working out $f \times m$, i.e. 20, 37.5, 25, 87.5
M1 Working out the total ÷ 20, i.e. 170 ÷ 20
Q1 £8.50

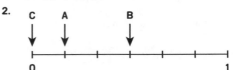
Money notation must be correct.

Probability (pages 76–77)

1. **B1** **(a)** Even chance
B1 **(b)** Unlikely

2.

C   A   B

0   1

B3 Fully correct **(B1 for each correct answer)**

3. **M1** **(a)** 1 − 0.25 − 0.3
A1 0.45
M1 **(b)** 0.3 × 40
A1 12 white counters

4. **M1** **(a)** $x = 1 − 0.2 − 0.1 − 0.4$
A1 $x = 0.3$
M1 **(b)** 0.4 × 200
A1 80

5. **B2** **(a)** $\frac{2}{9}$ **(B1 for correct numerator of 2 or correct denominator of 9)**
M1 **(b)** $1 − \frac{2}{9}$ or $\frac{3}{9} + \frac{4}{9}$
A1 $\frac{7}{9}$

6. **B2** **(a)** $\frac{1}{6}$ **(B1 for correct numerator of 1 or correct denominator of 6)**
M1 **(b)** $1 − \frac{2}{6}$ or $\frac{1}{6} + \frac{3}{6}$
A1 $\frac{4}{6}$ or $\frac{2}{3}$

Further Probability (pages 78–79)

1. **(a)**

		Dice					
		1	2	3	4	5	6
Coin	Head (H)	H1	H2	H3	H4	H5	H6
	Tail (T)	T1	T2	T3	T4	T5	T6

B2 Fully correct **(B1 for each correct row)**
B1 **(b)** $\frac{1}{12}$

2. **(a)**

		Spinner A		
		1	2	3
Spinner B	2	3	4	5
	4	5	6	7
	6	7	8	9

B2 Fully correct table **(B1 for four or five correct values)**
B2 **(b)** $\frac{2}{9}$ **(B1 for correct numerator of 2 or correct denominator of 9)**
M1 **(c)** $\frac{1}{3} \times 20$
A1 6.6…
Q1 6 or 7

The answer must be a whole number because the context is games.

3. **M1** If spinner is fair, you would expect it to land on number 1,

$\frac{1}{4} \times 60 = 15$ times; land on number 2, $\frac{1}{2} \times 60 = 30$ times; land on number 3, $\frac{1}{4} \times 60 = 15$ times **(Mark given for any correct statement)**

Q1 Conclusion with a valid reason, e.g. fair as all are close to the expected numbers or not fair as not exactly as expected.

A reason must be given to gain the quality of written communication mark.

4. **B1** **(a)** $\frac{78}{300}$ or $\frac{39}{150}$ or $\frac{13}{50}$ or $\frac{26}{100}$ or 0.26

M1 **(b)** $78 \div 300 \times 40$ or $62 \div 300 \times 40$ or $160 \div 300 \times 40$

M1 10.4 or 8.3 or 21.3, or 10 or 11 black, or 8 or 9 white, or 21 or 22 red

Q1 Values chosen that have a total of 40, e.g. 10, 8, 22 or 11, 8, 21

As you are told there are 40 counters in the bag, the total must add up to 40 to gain the quality of written communication mark.

(a) Which shape is congruent to shape B?

Answer: _____ *(1 mark)*

(b) Which other **two** shapes are congruent?

Answer: _____ *(1 mark)*

(c) Which **two** shapes are similar?

Answer: _____ *(1 mark)*

4. On the isometric grid draw a cuboid with length 4 units, width 3 units and height 2 units.

(2 marks)

5. Complete the table.

	Faces	Edges	Vertices
Cuboid	6		
Square-based Pyramid		8	

(4 marks)

6. Triangles *ABC* and *LMN* are congruent.

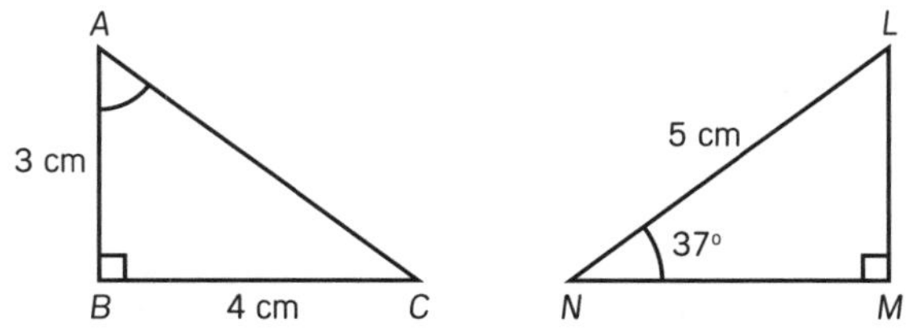

A — 3 cm — B — 4 cm — C

5 cm, 37°, L, N, M

Not drawn accurately

(a) Write down the length of *LM*.

Answer: _____ cm *(1 mark)*

(b) Work out angle *A*.

_____

Answer: _____ degrees *(2 marks)*

(Total: _____ / 16 marks)

Angles and Parallel Lines

1.

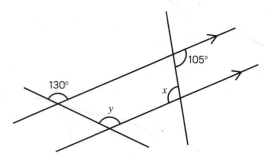

Not drawn accurately

(a) Write down the value of x.

Answer: _____ degrees   *(1 mark)*

(b) (i) Write down the value of y.

Answer: _____ degrees   *(1 mark)*

(ii) Give a reason for your answer.

_____   *(1 mark)*

2.

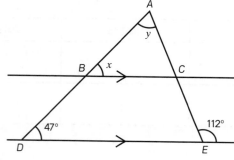

Not drawn accurately

(a) Write down the value of x.

Answer: _____ degrees   *(1 mark)*

(b) Work out the value of y.

_____

_____

Answer: _____ degrees   *(3 marks)*

3. Work out the value of x.

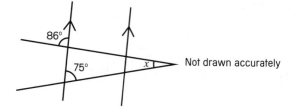

Not drawn accurately

_____

Answer: _____ degrees   *(2 marks)*

4. Triangle *ABC* is isosceles.

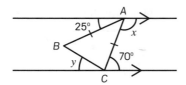

Not drawn accurately

(a) Work out the value of x.

Answer: .... degrees   *(2 marks)*

(b) Work out the value of y.

Answer: .... degrees   *(4 marks)*

5.

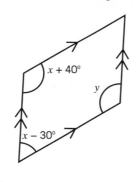

Not drawn accurately

(a) Work out the value of x.

Answer: .... degrees   *(4 marks)*

(b) Work out the value of y.

Answer: .... degrees   *(2 marks)*

(Total: .... / 21 marks)

Angles of Polygons

1.

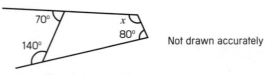

Not drawn accurately

(a) Work out the size of the angle marked x.

....

....

Answer: .... degrees   *(2 marks)*

(b) Give reasons for your answer.

....

....   *(1 mark)*

2. In this quadrilateral the sizes of the angles, in degrees, are $3x$, $2x$, $100°$ and $x + 20°$.

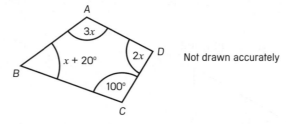

Not drawn accurately

(a) Use this information to write down an equation in terms of x.

....

Answer: ....   *(2 marks)*

(b) Work out the value of x.

....

....

Answer: .... degrees   *(2 marks)*

3. The diagram shows part of a regular polygon.

Not drawn accurately

(a) What is the size of each exterior angle of the polygon?

....

Answer: .... degrees   *(2 marks)*

(b) How many sides does the polygon have?

....

....

Answer: ....

(2 marks)

4. The diagram shows a regular hexagon and two squares.

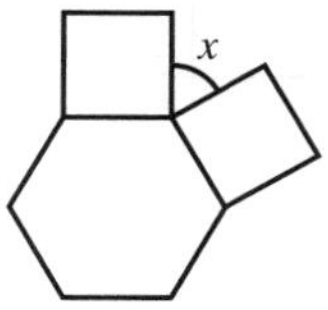

Not drawn accurately

Work out the value of x.

....

....

....

....

Answer: .... degrees

(4 marks)

5. The diagram shows a regular hexagon joined to a regular octagon.

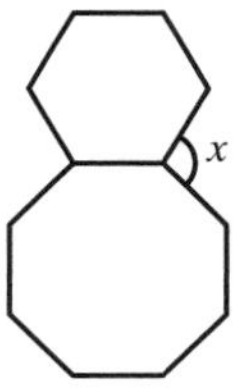

Not drawn accurately

Work out the value of x.

....

....

....

....

Answer: .... degrees

(4 marks)

(Total: .... / 19 marks)

Perimeter and Area

1. Here are two shapes A and B on a centimetre square grid:

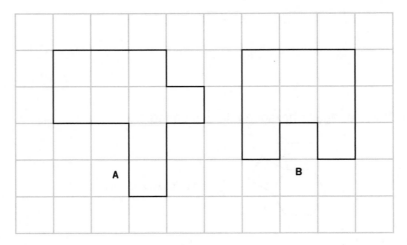

*(a) Which has the greater area? You **must** show your working.

_____

_____

Answer: _____ (3 marks)

*(b) Which has the greater perimeter? You **must** show your working.

_____

_____

Answer: _____ (3 marks)

2. This shape is drawn on a centimetre square grid:

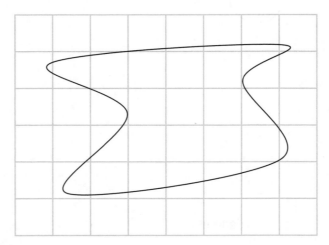

Estimate the area.

Answer: _____ cm² (2 marks)

3. **(a)** On the grid draw a net of this cuboid.

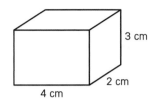

3 cm

Not drawn accurately

2 cm

4 cm

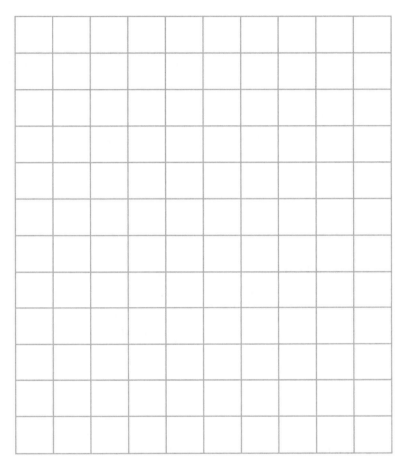

(2 marks)

(b) Work out the total surface area of the cuboid.

Answer: .... cm² *(3 marks)*

4. Sketch a net of a square-based pyramid on a separate piece of paper. *(1 mark)*

(Total: .... **/ 14 marks)**

Areas of Triangles and Quadrilaterals

 1. Work out the area of this triangle.

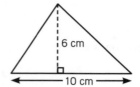

6 cm

10 cm

Not drawn accurately

Answer: _____ cm²   *(2 marks)*

2. Work out the area of this trapezium.

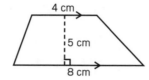

4 cm

5 cm

8 cm

Not drawn accurately

Answer: _____ cm²   *(2 marks)*

3. Work out the area of this parallelogram.

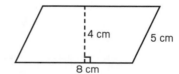

4 cm

5 cm

8 cm

Not drawn accurately

Answer: _____ cm²   *(2 marks)*

4. The diagram shows a picture frame.

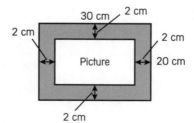

30 cm   2 cm

2 cm

2 cm

Picture   20 cm

2 cm

Not drawn accurately

Work out the area of the frame.

Answer: _____ cm²   *(3 marks)*

5. *ABCD* is a rectangle.

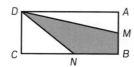

Not drawn accurately

M is the midpoint of *AB*. *N* is the midpoint of *BC*. What fraction of the area of *ABCD* is shaded?

....

....

Answer: ....

(3 marks)

6. The diagram shows two triangles with the same area.

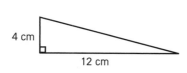 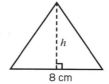

Not drawn accurately

Work out the height h.

....

....

....

Answer: .... cm

(3 marks)

7. This shape is made from a rectangle and a triangle. The height of the rectangle is twice the height of the triangle.

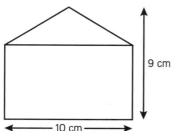

9 cm

Not drawn accurately

10 cm

Work out the area of the shape.

....

....

....

....

Answer: .... cm²

(4 marks)

(Total: .... / 19 marks)

Circumference and Area of Circles

1. Work out the circumference of a circle of radius 10 cm. Give your answer in terms of π.

Answer: .... cm *(2 marks)*

2. Work out the area of a circle of radius 6 cm.

Answer: .... cm^2 *(2 marks)*

3. Work out the area of a circle of radius 7 cm. Give your answer in terms of π.

Answer: .... cm^2 *(2 marks)*

4. The diagram shows a semicircle of radius 5.1 cm.

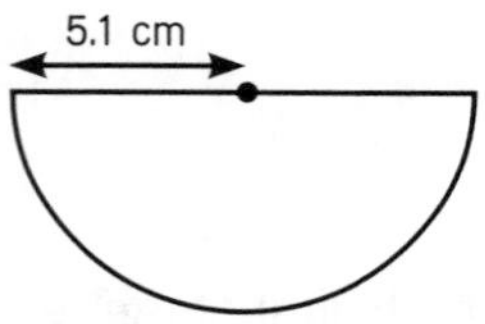

Not drawn accurately

Work out the perimeter.

Answer: .... cm *(3 marks)*

5. The diagram shows a quarter circle.

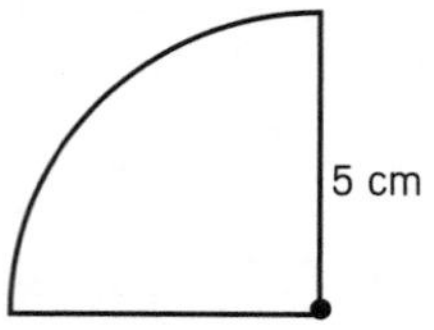

5 cm

Not drawn accurately

Work out the area of the quarter circle.

Answer: _____ cm² *(3 marks)*

6. The diagram shows a path around a circular garden.

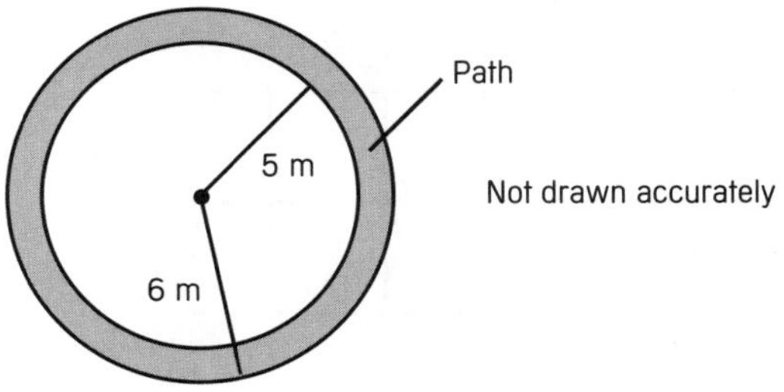

Path

5 m

Not drawn accurately

6 m

Work out the area of the path.

Answer: _____ m² *(3 marks)*

7. A wheel has radius 30 cm.

How far does it travel if it turns through 1000 complete revolutions?

Give your answer in metres to the nearest metre.

Answer: _____ m *(4 marks)*

(Total: _____ / 19 marks)

Plan and Elevation

 1. The diagram shows a solid made from six cubes.

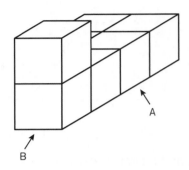

(a) On this grid draw the view from A.

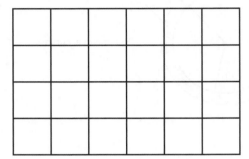

(1 mark)

(b) On this grid draw the view from B.

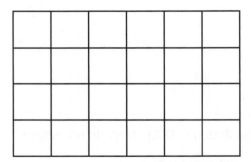

(1 mark)

 2. Here are the front elevation, side elevation and plan view of a 3-D shape:

Front Elevation	Side Elevation	Plan View
		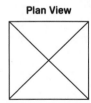

Draw a sketch of the 3-D shape.

(2 marks)

Plan and Elevation

Plan and Elevation

GEOMETRY & MEASURES

 3. Here are the three views of a 3-D shape:

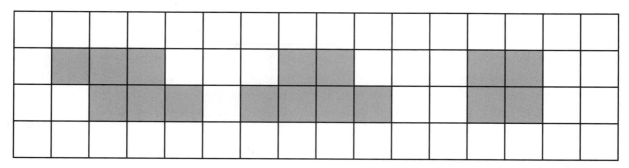

Plan View — Front Elevation — Side Elevation

Draw the 3-D shape on the isometric grid provided.

(2 marks)

 4. This shape is made from eight cubes.

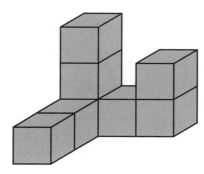

On the grid provided draw the **plan view**, **front elevation** and the **side elevation**.

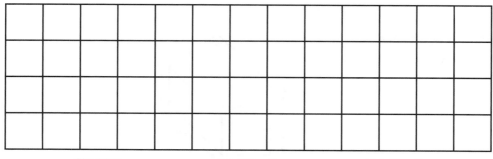

Plan View — Front Elevation — Side Elevation

(3 marks)

(Total: ..../ 9 marks)

© Lonsdale 53

Volumes of Prisms

1. Work out the volume of the cuboid.

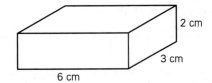

Answer: _____ cm³ (2 marks)

2. **(a)** Work out the area of the triangular cross-section of this prism.

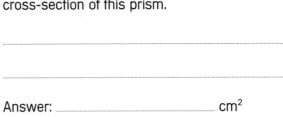

_____

_____

Answer: _____ cm² (2 marks)

(b) Work out the volume of this prism.

_____

Answer: _____ cm³ (2 marks)

3. Work out the volume of this prism.

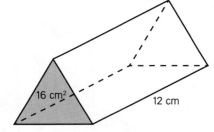

_____

_____

Answer: _____ cm³ (2 marks)

4. The diagram shows a shed in the shape of a prism.

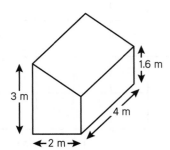

Work out the volume of the shed.

Answer: _____ m³

(3 marks)

5. Work out the volume of the cylinder.

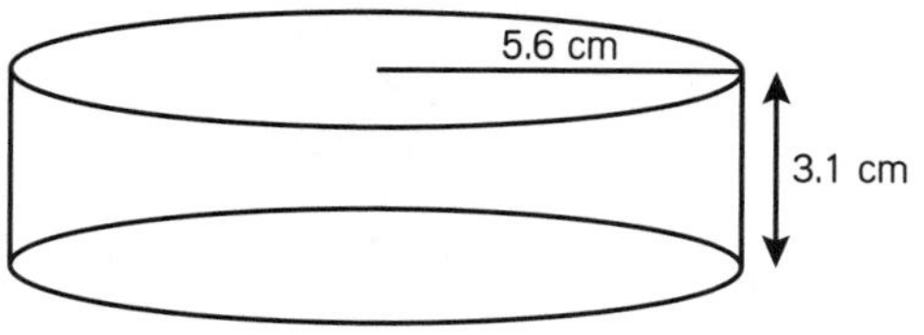

5.6 cm

3.1 cm

Answer: _____ cm³

(2 marks)

6. The diagram shows a T-shaped steel girder.

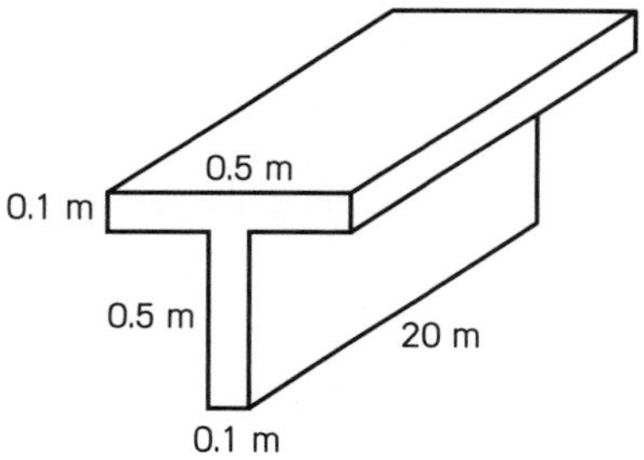

0.1 m

0.5 m

0.5 m

20 m

0.1 m

(a) Work out the volume of steel in the girder.

Answer: _____ m³

(4 marks)

*(b) How many of these girders can be made from 15 m³ of steel?

Answer: _____

(3 marks)

(Total: _____ / 20 marks)

Pythagoras' Theorem

 1. *ABC* is a right-angled triangle.

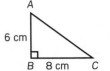

6 cm

B 8 cm *C*

A

Not drawn accurately

Work out the length *AC*.

_____

_____

_____

Answer: _____ cm

(3 marks)

2. *ABC* is a right-angled triangle.

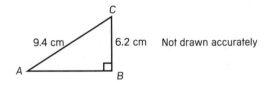

C

9.4 cm 6.2 cm Not drawn accurately

A *B*

Work out the length *AB*. Give your answer to 1 decimal place.

_____

_____

_____

Answer: _____ cm

(4 marks)

3. Work out the length of the diagonal of this rectangle. Give your answer to 1 decimal place.

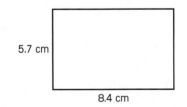

5.7 cm

8.4 cm

Not drawn accurately

_____

_____

_____

Answer: _____ cm

(4 marks)

4. The diagram shows a rectangular field with a straight path between two gates.

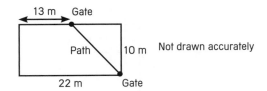

Work out the length of the path.

....

....

....

Answer: .... m   (4 marks)

5. The diagram shows a five-metre ladder against a wall.

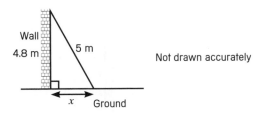

Work out the distance, x metres, of the ladder from the foot of the wall.

....

....

Answer: .... m   (3 marks)

6. A ship sails 4 km due North. It then sails 7.5 km due East. It then sails directly back to the port.

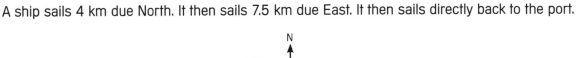

The speed of the ship is 10 km per hour. Work out the total time taken for the ship's journey.

....

....

....

....

Answer: .... hours   (5 marks)

(Total: .... / 23 marks)

Transformations

1.

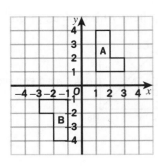

(a) Reflect shape A in the x-axis.

Label it C. *(2 marks)*

(b) Describe fully the **single** transformation that takes shape A to shape B.

_____

_____ *(3 marks)*

2.

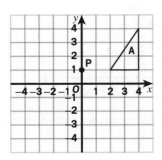

(a) Rotate triangle A through 180° about point P.

Label the new triangle B. *(2 marks)*

(b) Translate triangle A by the vector $\begin{pmatrix} -1 \\ -3 \end{pmatrix}$.

Label the new triangle C. *(1 mark)*

3. Reflect triangle A in the line $y = -x$

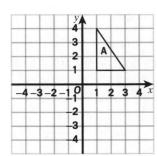

(2 marks)

4.

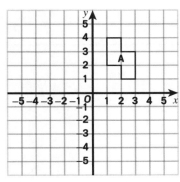

(a) Translate shape A by the vector $\begin{pmatrix} 1 \\ -4 \end{pmatrix}$.

   Label the new shape B. *(2 marks)*

(b) Reflect shape A in the line $x = -1$

   Label the new shape C. *(2 marks)*

5. Enlarge triangle A by scale factor 3, centre (0, 0).

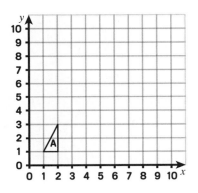

(3 marks)

6.

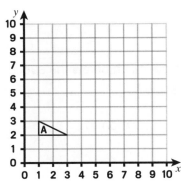

Triangle A is reflected in the line $x = 4$ to give triangle B. Triangle B is reflected in the line $y = 3$ to give triangle C.

Describe the **single** transformation that takes triangle A to triangle C.

_____

_____ *(3 marks)*

(Total: _____ / 20 marks)

Basic Measures

1. **(a)** Measure the line AB.

A ————————————————— B

Answer: _____ cm

(1 mark)

(b) Measure the angle shown.

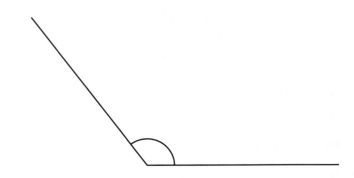

Answer: _____ degrees

(1 mark)

2. How much water is in the cylinder?

Answer: _____ ml

(1 mark)

300 ml

200 ml

100 ml

0 ml

3. **(a)** The speed limit is 40 mph. How much **below** the speed limit does the speedometer show?

Answer: _____ mph

(1 mark)

(b) How much fuel is in the tank?
Give your answer as a fraction of a tank.

Answer: _____

(1 mark)

4. **(a)** Use the scale on the jug to change 2 litres to pints.

Answer: _____ pints   *(1 mark)*

(b) Use the scale to change 1 pint to litres.

Answer: _____ litres   *(1 mark)*

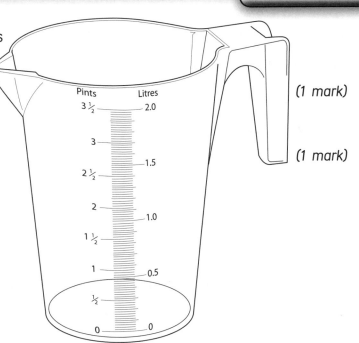

 5. **(a)** Measure the angle marked x.

Answer: _____ degrees   *(1 mark)*

(b) Use your answer to part **(a)** to work out the size of the angle marked y.

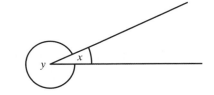

_____

Answer: _____ degrees   *(2 marks)*

 6. Here is part of a bus timetable:

Rotherham Interchange	1008	1038	1108
Hospital	1019	1049	1119
Bramley	1039	1109	1139

(a) How long does it take to get from Rotherham Interchange to the hospital?

Answer: _____ minutes   *(1 mark)*

(b) My home is 15 minutes' walk from the Interchange. I want to catch a bus to Bramley to arrive before midday. What is the latest time that I can set off from home?

_____

Answer: _____   *(2 marks)*

(Total: _____ **/ 13 marks)**

Conversion and Estimation

1. Write down a suitable metric unit for:

(a) the length of a classroom.

Answer: _____ *(1 mark)*

(b) the weight of an adult.

Answer: _____ *(1 mark)*

(c) the capacity of a fuel tank.

Answer: _____ *(1 mark)*

2. Kirk is going to New York on business.

He changes £700 into dollars. The exchange rate is £1 = $1.58

(a) How many dollars does he get?

_____

_____

Answer: $ _____ *(2 marks)*

(b) When Kirk returns to London he still has $230 left, which he changes back to pounds. The exchange rate is now £1 = $1.75

How much does he get back? Give your answer to the nearest pound.

_____

_____

Answer: £ _____ *(2 marks)*

3. **(a)** Complete the following sentence.

5 miles is approximately _____ kilometres. *(1 mark)*

(b) Use your answer to part **(a)** to change 60 miles to kilometres.

_____

_____

Answer: _____ km *(2 marks)*

Conversion and Estimation

GEOMETRY & MEASURES

4. **(a)** Complete each conversion using one of these numbers.

| 1.75 | 2.2 | 2.5 | 4.5 | 16 | 30 |

The first one has been done for you.

1 gallon is approximately 4.5 litres.

1 kilogram is approximately ＿＿＿＿＿＿＿＿＿＿＿ pounds.

1 inch is approximately ＿＿＿＿＿＿＿＿＿＿＿ centimetres.

10 miles is approximately ＿＿＿＿＿＿＿＿＿＿＿ kilometres.

(2 marks)

(b) Convert 90 litres into gallons.

＿＿＿＿＿＿＿＿＿＿＿＿＿＿＿＿＿＿＿＿＿＿＿＿＿＿＿

＿＿＿＿＿＿＿＿＿＿＿＿＿＿＿＿＿＿＿＿＿＿＿＿＿＿＿

Answer: ＿＿＿＿＿＿＿＿＿＿＿ gallons

(2 marks)

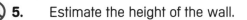

5. Estimate the height of the wall.

＿＿＿＿＿＿＿＿＿＿＿＿＿＿＿＿＿＿＿＿＿＿＿＿＿＿＿

＿＿＿＿＿＿＿＿＿＿＿＿＿＿＿＿＿＿＿＿＿＿＿＿＿＿＿

Answer: ＿＿＿＿＿＿＿＿＿＿＿ m

(3 marks)

(Total: ＿＿＿＿ /17 marks)

1. On a separate piece of paper, use a ruler and compasses to construct a triangle with sides 5 cm, 6 cm and 7 cm. *(2 marks)*

 2. The diagram shows a sketch of triangle *ABC*.

AB = 9 cm

AC = 5 cm

Angle A = 47°

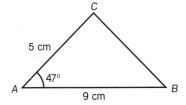

Not drawn accurately

Make an accurate drawing of triangle *ABC* on a separate piece of paper. *(2 marks)*

 3. Construct the perpendicular bisector of the line *AB*.

(2 marks)

 4. The diagram shows a sketch of triangle *ABC*.

AB = 7.5 cm

Angle A = 38°

Angle B = 95°

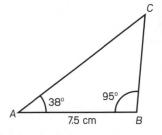

Not drawn accurately

Make an accurate drawing of triangle *ABC* on a separate piece of paper. *(2 marks)*

5. Use a ruler and a pair of compasses to construct the bisector of angle *A*.

Show clearly all your construction arcs.

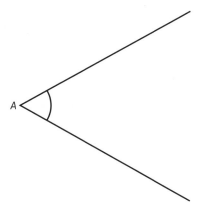

(2 marks)

 6. A sketch of an isosceles triangle is shown.

(a) On a separate piece of paper, construct an isosceles triangle that has two sides of 6 cm and an angle of 40° between them. *(3 marks)*

(b) Measure the base.

Answer: _____ cm *(1 mark)*

 7. Construct an equilateral triangle. The base line has been drawn for you.

_____

(2 marks)

(Total: _____ / 16 marks)

Bearings and Loci

1. The diagram shows the position of two ships, A and B.

   (a) Measure the size of the angle marked x.

   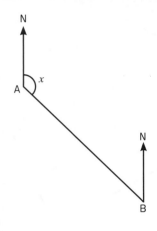

   Scale: 1 cm represents 20 km

   Answer: _____ °   *(1 mark)*

   (b) Work out the actual distance between the two ships.

   _____

   Answer: _____ km   *(2 marks)*

   (c) Ship B is sailing towards ship A. Work out the three-figure bearing of A from B.

   _____

   Answer: _____ °   *(2 marks)*

2. On the map A is a town. B is 12 km from A on a bearing of 050°. C is 8 km from A on a bearing of 340°.

   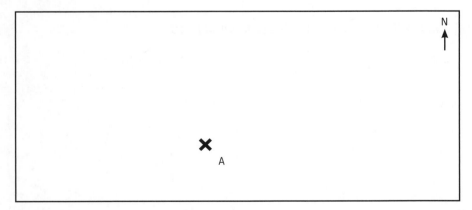

   Scale: 1 cm represents 4 km

   (a) Mark the positions of B and C on the map.   *(4 marks)*

   (b) Work out the actual distance of B from C.

   _____

   Answer: _____ km   *(2 marks)*

3. The diagram shows a garden with a wall along one edge.

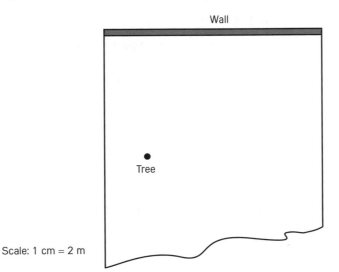

Scale: 1 cm = 2 m

Jack wants to build a pond in the garden so that it is at least 2 metres from the wall and more than 5 metres from the tree. On the diagram, shade the region where the pond could be built. *(3 marks)*

4. The diagram shows a garden next to a house.

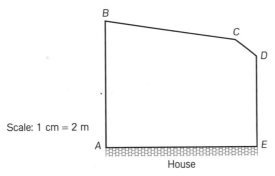

Scale: 1 cm = 2 m

Lucy wants to plant a tree in the garden so that it is closer to *B* than *E* and it is more than 3 metres from the house. On the diagram, shade the region where the tree could be planted. *(4 marks)*

5. The diagram shows a goat tied to a post in a field. The goat can reach 8 metres from the post. On the diagram draw the locus of the shape the goat can reach.

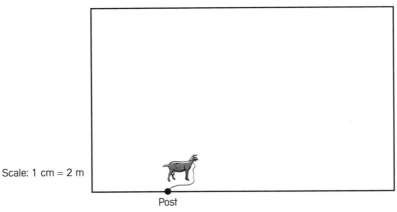

Scale: 1 cm = 2 m

Post

(2 marks)

(Total: .... / 20 marks)

Handling Data Cycle and Questionnaires

1. A teacher gives her students this question.

   How many times do you exercise each week?

   1 to 2 ☐   3 to 5 ☐   5 to 7 ☐   More than 8 ☐

   Write down **two** things that are wrong with this question.

   ....

   ....

   .... *(2 marks)*

2. Write a question to find out the number of people in a family. Include a response section.

   ....

   ....

   .... *(2 marks)*

3. Amir wants to find out how much people spent on Christmas presents. He uses this question on a questionnaire.

   How much did you spend on Christmas presents?

   Less than £5 ☐   £5 to £10 ☐   £10 to £15 ☐   More than £15 ☐

   (a) Write down **two** things that are wrong with this question.

   ....

   ....

   .... *(2 marks)*

   (b) Design a better question to find out how much people spent on presents. Include a response section.

   ....

   ....

   .... *(2 marks)*

   (c) Amir asks his question to 10 children while standing outside a toy shop.

   Give **two** reasons why this might not be suitable.

   ....

   ....

   .... *(2 marks)*

Handling Data Cycle and Questionnaires

4. Mrs Smith wants to find out what people think of the service in her shop. She uses this question on her questionnaire.

What do you think of the service in my shop?

Outstanding ☐   Good ☐   Satisfactory ☐

(a) Write down **one** thing that is wrong with this question.

....

....

(1 mark)

(b) Design a suitable question to find out how often people use the shop. Include a response section.

....

....

(2 marks)

*5. Use the handling data cycle to describe how you would test the following hypothesis.

January is the coldest month of the year.

....

....

....

....

....

(3 marks)

*6. Use the handling data cycle to describe how you would test the following hypothesis.

Girls in year 9 are better at mathematics than boys in year 9.

....

....

....

....

....

(3 marks)

(Total: .... / 19 marks)

Averages and Range

1. 10 students were asked how many hours of revision they did last night. Their answers were:

1	0	1	3	3	1	2	1	4	2

(a) Write down the mode.

Answer: .... *(1 mark)*

(b) Work out the median.

_____

Answer: .... *(2 marks)*

*(c) The data for an extra student is now included. She did three hours of revision.

How will this affect the median? You **must** give reasons for your answer.

_____

_____ *(2 marks)*

2. The table shows the number of eggs laid by some hens in a week. Calculate the mean number of eggs laid per hen.

Number of Eggs	Number of Hens
0	2
1	4
2	5
3	6
4	13

_____

_____

_____

Answer: .... *(3 marks)*

3. The table shows the time taken by the school bus to get to school over 20 days.

Time Taken, t (minutes)	Frequency
$15 < t \leqslant 20$	4
$20 < t \leqslant 25$	10
$25 < t \leqslant 30$	6

Work out an estimate for the mean journey time.

Answer: .... minutes   *(4 marks)*

4.   The table shows the heights of 30 students in a class.

Height, h (metres)	Frequency
$1.2 < h \leqslant 1.4$	4
$1.4 < h \leqslant 1.6$	7
$1.6 < h \leqslant 1.8$	13
$1.8 < h \leqslant 2.0$	6

(a) Write down the modal class interval.

Answer: ....   *(1 mark)*

(b) Find the class interval that contains the median.

Answer: ....   *(1 mark)*

*(c) Trevor claims that his height of 1.55 metres is the mean.

Explain how you can tell that he must be wrong. You do not have to calculate the estimated mean.

....

....

....   *(1 mark)*

5.   Write down five numbers that have a mean of 10 and a range of 10.

....

....

Answer: ....   *(2 marks)*

(Total: .... / 17 marks)

Collecting and Sorting Data

1. A travel agent gives a survey to 20 customers. The survey asks how many holidays the customers take each year. Here are the results:

2	1	3	4	1	1	2	1	2	1
3	2	1	1	2	2	1	1	3	1

(a) Give a reason why none of the customers said zero.

_____ *(1 mark)*

(b) Complete the table.

Number of Holidays	Tally	Frequency
1		
2		
3		
4		

(2 marks)

2. The marks for 15 students in a geography test are shown.

2	1	1	5					
3	0	0	3	4	7	8	8	9
4	2	4	7	9				

Key: 2 | 1   represents a mark of 21

(a) Write down the median mark.

Answer: _____ *(1 mark)*

(b) Work out the range of the marks.

_____

Answer: _____ *(1 mark)*

(c) The 15 students also took a history test. The median mark for history was 34. The range of the history marks was 17.

Use this information to compare the marks in geography and history.

_____

_____ *(2 marks)*

*3. The ages of 11 people in a band are shown.

15   14   18   18   19   13   9   21   8   21   24

Complete the ordered stem-and-leaf diagram to show these ages.

0 |

1 |

2 | Key: *(4 marks)*

4. The table shows information about some patients at a doctor's surgery.

	Male	Female
Adults	43	81
Children	24	22

(a) How many more female patients are there than male patients?

Answer: ....   *(2 marks)*

(b) A patient is chosen at random. What is the probability that it is a female child?

Answer: ....   *(2 marks)*

5. 30 children are asked what type of TV programmes they prefer. There are twice as many boys as girls.

- Three times more girls than boys chose soaps.

- The same number of girls and boys chose comedies.

- 2 girls chose cartoons.

- 10 children chose comedies.

Use this information to complete the two-way table.

	Soaps	Comedies	Cartoons	Total
Girls			2	
Boys				
Total		10		30

(4 marks)

(Total: .... / 19 marks)

Representing Data

1. The table shows the number of year 11 students late for school one week.

Monday	Tuesday	Wednesday	Thursday	Friday
12	6	7	8	4

Complete the pictogram for the data. Monday is already completed.

Key: ⊗ represents _____ students

Monday	⊗ ⊗
Tuesday	
Wednesday	
Thursday	
Friday	

(3 marks)

2. The bar chart shows the car sales for a garage in one month.

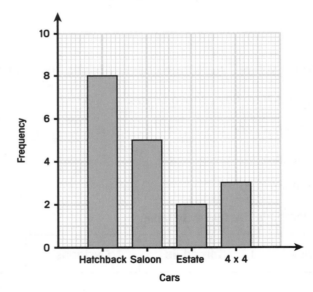

(a) How many hatchbacks were sold?

Answer: _____ *(1 mark)*

(b) How many cars were sold altogether?

Answer: _____ *(1 mark)*

3. The table shows the marks for 10 students in two mathematics tests.

Test 1	35	46	50	20	17	38	46	30	10	41
Test 2	24	30	50	23	20	34	42	30	12	39

(a) Plot the data as a scatter
diagram using the grid provided. *(2 marks)*

(b) Draw a line of best fit. *(1 mark)*

(c) Describe the correlation.

....

....

.... *(1 mark)*

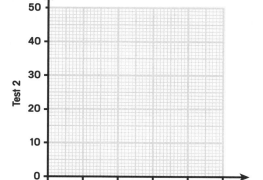

(d) Another student scored 25 marks on Test 1 but missed
Test 2. Estimate her mark on Test 2.

Answer: .... *(2 marks)*

4. The table shows the amounts spent by 20 customers in a shop.

Amount Spent, £A	Frequency
$0 < A \leq 5$	8
$5 < A \leq 10$	5
$10 < A \leq 15$	2
$15 < A \leq 20$	5

(a) Draw a frequency polygon to show this
information using the grid provided. *(3 marks)*

*(b) Calculate an estimate of the mean amount
spent by the 20 customers.

....

....

....

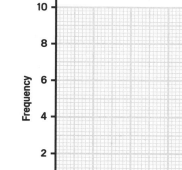

Answer: £ .... *(4 marks)*

(Total: .... / 18 marks)

Probability

1. Here are eight cards:

Describe the chance of the following events using one of these options:

Certain   **Impossible**   **Likely**   **Unlikely**   **Even chance**

(a) Choosing a card with a 3 on it.

Answer: ....   *(1 mark)*

(b) Choosing a card with a 4 on it.

Answer: ....   *(1 mark)*

2. An ordinary, fair six-sided dice is rolled.

On the probability scale mark and label the probability of:

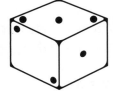

A The dice landing on the number 3

B The dice landing on a number greater than 3

C The dice landing on a number greater than 6

0   1   *(3 marks)*

3. A bag contains only black, white and green counters.

The table shows the probabilities that a counter chosen at random is a black counter or a white counter.

Colour	Black	White	Green
Probability	0.25	0.3	

(a) Work out the probability that a counter chosen at random is green.

....

Answer: ....   *(2 marks)*

(b) There are 40 counters in the bag. Work out the number of white counters.

....

Answer: ....   *(2 marks)*

4. Here is a biased spinner:

The probability that the spinner will land on each of the numbers 1, 2 and 3 is shown.

Number	1	2	3	4
Probability	0.2	0.1	0.4	x

(a) Work out the value of x.

Answer: ....

(2 marks)

(b) The spinner is spun 200 times. Work out the number of times you would expect it to land on the number 3.

Answer: ....

(2 marks)

 5. In a box there are 3 blue pens, 2 black pens and 4 red pens. Gary takes a pen at random from the box.

(a) Write down the probability that it is a black pen.

Answer: ....

(2 marks)

(b) Work out the probability that it is a blue or a red pen.

Answer: ....

(2 marks)

 6. There are only blue, red and yellow counters in a bag. The ratio of blue to red to yellow is 2 : 1 : 3

(a) What is the probability that a counter chosen at random is red?

Answer: ....

(2 marks)

(b) What is the probability that a counter chosen at random is **not** blue?

Answer: ....

(2 marks)

(Total: .... / 21 marks)

Further Probability

1. A fair coin is thrown and an ordinary fair dice is rolled.

    (a) Complete the sample space diagram.

Dice

		1	2	3	4	5	6
Coin	**Head (H)**	H1	H2				
	Tail (T)	T1					

(2 marks)

    (b) Work out the probability of a head and a 6.

    Answer: ....   *(1 mark)*

2. Here are two fair spinners. The numbers each spinner lands on are added to get the score.

Spinner A   Spinner B

    (a) Complete the table.

Spinner A

		1	2	3
Spinner B	**2**	3		
	4		6	
	6			9

(2 marks)

    (b) Work out the probability of a score of 5.

    Answer: ....   *(2 marks)*

*(c) In a game, a player wins if the score is even and loses if the score is odd.

Harriet plays 20 games. Estimate the number of games she wins.

Answer: ....

(3 marks)

*3. This spinner is spun 60 times. Here are the results:

Score	1	2	3
Frequency	18	28	14

Do you think the spinner is fair? Give a reason for your answer.

(2 marks)

4. A bag contains 40 counters. The counters are black, white or red.

A counter is taken at random from the bag, the colour is recorded and then the counter is put back in the bag. This is repeated 300 times. The results are:

Black	White	Red
78	62	160

(a) What is the relative frequency of picking a black counter?

Answer: ....

(1 mark)

*(b) How many counters of each colour do you think are in the bag?

Answer: ....

(3 marks)

(Total: .... **/ 16 marks)**

Formulae Sheet

Area of trapezium $= \frac{1}{2}(a + b)h$

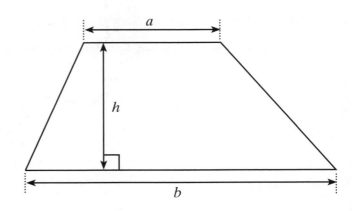

Volume of prism = area of cross-section × length

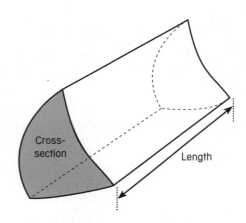